# OUT of the SHADOWS

*Local community action and the European Community*

EF/92/12/EN

Gabriel Chanan is Director of Research at the Community Development Foundation, UK. Set up in 1968, CDF pioneers, analyses and disseminates new forms of community development, with the aim of ensuring effective participation of people in determining the conditions in which they live. CDF works through local action projects, research, policy analysis, information, consultancy and dissemination. Over the past five years it has taken a leading role in networking with other European bodies in this field and developing the application of community development experience to European dimensions of social policy. Gabriel Chanan has also written widely on issues in education and the arts.

European Foundation
for the Improvement of
Living and Working Conditions

# OUT of the SHADOWS
*Local community action and the European Community*

Final report of the research project
Coping with Social and Economic Change
at Neighbourhood Level

*Gabriel Chanan*
Community Development Foundation

Loughlinstown House, Shankill, Co. Dublin, Ireland
Tel: 282 68 88 Fax: 282 64 56 Telex: 30726 EURF EI

Cataloguing data can be found at the end of this publication

Luxembourg: Office for Official Publications of the European Communities, 1992

ISBN 92-826-4146-5

© European Foundation for the Improvement of Living and Working Conditions, 1992.

For rights of translation or reproduction, applications should be made to the Director, European Foundation for the Improvement of Living and Working Conditions, Loughlinstown House, Shankill, Co. Dublin, Ireland.

*Printed in Ireland*

*PREFACE*

This report signals the end of an extensive research programme, "Coping with social and economic change at neighbourhood level", initiated by the Foundation in 1987. Local community action and the active involvement of people living in urban areas was identified as an emerging issue in the Foundation's review from 1985 on "Living Conditions in Urban Areas". Local action on a whole range of economic, social and environmental problems was of growing interest at city level but also in relation to national and European Community programmes concerned with social and economic development.

Demographic change, economic restructuring, large-scale unemployment, new technologies and political and institutional developments, have led to changes in the resources, options and capabilities of people, households and localities across Europe. In developing this Foundation research programme, three related issues have been the basis for the work. These are:

1) *social and spatial polarisation* The processes of social, economic and political change have produced uneven social and spatial effects, giving rise to an accumulation of negative consequences for certain categories of people and households in particular communities. These include concentrations of poverty and unemployment among households headed by older and unskilled persons, young people with few skills or educational qualifications, women, single parent households and ethnic minorities. Such concentrations are often found spatially concentrated in inner cities and on the periphery of large urban areas.

2) *the changing nature of social policy and modes of welfare provision* The last ten years have seen what has become known as the crisis of the welfare state and an increasing development of partnerships between the state, the private and voluntary sectors in the delivery of public services. Within these partnerships, the role of local groups and organisations has been a growing one, particularly in certain Member States.

3) *calls for economic and social cohesion.* With progress towards the Single Market, existing social and spatial disparities present increasing challenges to policy makers. There has been growing demand, including the latest developments emanating from Maastricht, to improve social and economic cohesion in Europe. One avenue being pursued is the development of the role of locally based action and initiatives to deal with these problems. Programmes at EC level, such as Poverty 3, LEDA and ERGO, are examples of this trend.

Evidently there are many benefits arising from these local initiatives, but there is also a danger that, through a combination of uncritical appraisal of their capabilities and a general concern to reduce social expenditure, they may become an overburdened means of addressing the social and economic problems of those most marginal in our society.

The Foundation's research programme set out to achieve a better understanding, on a European basis, of the capabilities and limitations of local community action in resolving social, economic and environmental problems in disadvantaged urban areas. It has been developed through a number of stages.

*Stage 1 (1987-89).* Research institutes from four Member States (Belgium, Ireland, Netherlands and United Kingdom) examined the relevant literature on local community action. They interviewed a sample of policy makers and practitioners to assess the thinking about neighbourhood and local community life, which lay behind policy developments. This resulted in four national reports, an annotated bibliography and a synthesis report, "Social Change and Local Action". This report clarified concepts and classification schemes, distinguished different forms of local action and illustrated how they worked in different settings. It also addressed critical questions about the scale and scope of local initiatives considering which problems they can address and under what conditions, who is likely to be involved and what resources are required.

*Stage 2 (1988-89).* During this period, the work was extended to include three additional Member States (Greece, Portugal and Spain) and the strategy and details for the field research work were developed. A seminar was held in Maastricht in June 1989 to debate the proposed research plan with researchers from across the European Community.

***Stage 3 (1990-92)***. Field research was undertaken involving households, local community organisations and policy makers in selected localities in all seven Member States. From the national reports, this synthesis report has been prepared. This was evaluated at a meeting held on 11 March 1992 in Brussels, to which representatives of the groups on the Foundation's Administrative Board were invited, namely employers, trade unions, governments and the European Commission. Representatives from the Economic and Social Committee, O.E.C.D. and AEDIL (European Association for Information on Local Development) were also invited to the meeting. The report was welcomed by the participants who felt it shed considerable light on how local action works, its strengths and weaknesses, and the importance of local groups in the development of social cohesion. The results were regarded as challenging to policy makers at all levels - European, regional, national and local. The need for full and extensive dissemination was stressed. Some recommendations were made to strengthen the report, particularly in updating it to take account of the results of the Maastricht summit.

This report was then approved for publication and support was expressed for the further programme of dissemination which will include a major European conference "Citizen Action - involving people at local level", to be held in Dublin on 23-25 September 1992.

*Wendy O'Conghaile*　　　　　　　　　　　　　　　　　　　　　　*Dublin, April 1992*

*Robert Anderson*

*'Apart from permanent associations such as townships, cities and counties created by law, there are a quantity of others whose existence and growth are solely due to the initiative of individuals. The inhabitant... is restless and defiant in his outlook towards the authority of society and appeals to its power only when he cannot do without it... If some obstacle blocks the public road, halting the circulation of traffic, the neighbours at once form a deliberative body; this improvised assembly produces an executive authority which remedies the trouble before anyone has thought of the possibility of some previously constituted authority beyond that of those concerned. Where enjoyment is concerned, people associate to make festivities grander and more orderly... Public security, trade and industry, morals and religion all provide the aims for associations. There is no end which the human will despairs of attaining by the free action of the collective power of individuals.'*

Alexis de Tocqueville, *Democracy in America* (1835)

# Contents

| | |
|---|---|
| List of tables | XI |
| Acknowledgements | XII |
| Introductory note | XIII |
| Executive summary | XV |

**Chapters**

## 1 What is local action? — 1

| | |
|---|---|
| INTRODUCTION | 1 |
| Fundamental yet hidden | 1 |
| Origins of the research | 2 |
| The focus of innovation | 2 |
| A distinct sector | 3 |
| HOW THE INVESTIGATION WAS CARRIED OUT | 5 |
| THE CONTEXT FOR LOCAL ACTION | 7 |
| More detailed questions | 7 |
| Intervention and the permanent partner | 10 |
| Importance of autonomy | 10 |
| The interface with public authorities | 11 |
| Definitions | 11 |
| THE CASE-STUDY LOCALITIES: | 17 |
| *Sluizeken and Muide*, Ghent, Belgium | 18 |
| *Perama*, Piraeus, Greece | 20 |
| *Tallaght*, Dublin, Ireland | 22 |
| *Amsterdam Mid-North*, Amsterdam, Netherlands | 24 |
| *Oliveira do Douro*, Oporto, Portugal | 26 |
| *Can Serra*, Barcelona, Spain | 28 |
| *Thamesmead*, London, United Kingdom | 30 |

## 2 People, localities and problems: the household survey — 33

| | |
|---|---|
| Introduction | 33 |
| The sample populations | 34 |
| Problems and issues | 37 |
| Methods of coping: responses to problems | 43 |
| Involvement in groups | 46 |
| General groups and social issue groups | 52 |
| Knowledge of issue groups and level of activity | 55 |
| Telephones | 55 |
| Sources of help and levels of satisfaction | 57 |

## 3 Local groups: what they do — 65
Introduction — 65
Local groups and local action — 65
Method — 66
Emerging contours of local groups sector — 67
Summary profiles of local groups sector — 68
'Focus' groups and policy issues — 71
Examples of achievements — 74
Quantification — 77
Complex effects — 78
Givers and receivers — 81
Participation: concentric circles — 84
The excluded — 85
Women and local groups — 86
Ethnic groups — 90

## 4 Local groups: how they function — 95
Autonomy — 95
Participation — 97
Professionalisation — 98
Resources — 99
Finding the right internal-external balance — 101
Umbrella organisations and community work — 102

## 5 Making policies for local action — 109
Common themes and national variations — 109
Groups and policies - connections and disconnections — 112
Policy-makers' views — 114
Funding and control: a basis for partnership? — 118

## 6 Conclusions and recommendations: making the most of local action — 125
Introduction — 125
The role of the European Community — 126
REVIEW OF NATIONAL CONCLUSIONS — 130
   The need for local action - and a government framework — 130
   Cautions — 131
   Decentralisation and local authorities — 131
   The local government framework — 132
   Towards co-ordinated local strategy — 133
   Dangers of incorporation — 135
GENERAL CONCLUSIONS — 137
   Fundamentals — 138
   Relationship with the voluntary sector — 138
   Relationship with poverty and disadvantage — 140
   Gender and unpaid work — 144
STRATEGIES FOR DEVELOPING LOCAL ACTION — 146
RECOMMENDATIONS — 152

## References — 156

# *List of tables*

| | | |
|---|---|---|
| 1.1 | Framework of definitions | 12 |
| | Map of the case study localities | 17 |
| | | |
| | Chapter 2 deals with the household survey | |
| 2.1 | Time of residence in locality | 36 |
| 2.2 | Unprompted issues | 37 |
| 2.3 | Prompted issues | 38 |
| 2.4 | Combined issues | 40 |
| 2.5 | Active on issues by locality | 43 |
| 2.6 | Active on issues by sex | 44 |
| 2.7 | Active on issues by age | 44 |
| 2.8 | Active on issues by time in locality | 45 |
| 2.9 | Involvement with groups | 47 |
| 2.10 | Variability of involvement in groups | 47 |
| 2.11 | Involvement in groups by sex | 49 |
| 2.12 | Involvement in groups by age | 49 |
| 2.13 | Involvement in groups by time in locality | 50 |
| 2.14 | Number of named groups known | 53 |
| 2.15 | Active on issues by knowledge of groups | 54 |
| 2.16 | Ownership of telephone | 56 |
| 2.17 | Active on issues by telephone ownership | 56 |
| 2.18 | Recourses for problems | 57 |
| 2.19 | Recourses for problems by locality | 58 |
| 2.20 | Satisfaction with recourses: local groups and organisations | 59 |
| 2.21 | Satisfaction with recourses: friends, relations and neighbours | 59 |
| 2.22 | Satisfaction with recourses: public authorities | 60 |
| 2.23 | Satisfaction with recourses: influential people | 60 |
| | | |
| 3.1 | Locality studies: summary profiles of local groups sectors | 68 |
| 3.2 | Local groups sectors: combined figures from the seven localities | 70 |
| 3.3 | Groups selected for in-depth study | 72 |
| 3.4 | The role of the Patients' Society in Bannedok and outside | 80 |
| 3.5 | Typology of immigrant associations by orientation | 91 |
| | | |
| 5.1 | Local community action: shifting the paradigm | 121 |
| 5.2 | Six partners to local action: strengths and weaknesses | 122 |

(XI)

# *Acknowledgements*

This report is the culmination of many research products on which it is based but which it does not supersede. It is in reality the product of the whole team of researchers and others who organised and produced the initial reports, research plans and in particular the seven national fieldwork reports. It has been a great privilege and pleasure to work with this team. Thanks therefore to John Bell, Patricia Boucneau, Marijke Declair, Yvonne Dhooge, Annemiek Harberink, Carmel Duggan, Dimitris Emmanuel, Jan Foolen, A. Monteiro, Rob Renier, Tom Ronayne, Fernanda Rodriguez, Gloria Rubiol, Ken Shanks, Anny Stevens, Stephen Stoer, Effie Stroussopoulou, Ricardo Suarez, P. Vieira, Koos Vos and Sien Winters. Wendy O'Conghaile and Robert Anderson from the European Foundation were a constant source of help and interpretation as well as overseeing the project. Experts who commented on drafts and attended discussion meetings are too varied to mention but special acknowledgement should be made to the 'Social Partner' representatives Bernard Le Marchand and Louis Buonaccorsi. I would like to add personal thanks to colleagues at the Community Development Foundation for encouragement and stimulus, particularly David Thomas, whose original concept led to the project, Paul Henderson and Charlie McConnell.
GC April '92

Photos by Kenneth Shanks
Statistical processing by John Bell
Design and layout by Dave Richards

**Shared vision: community artist and local residents plan a mural to brighten a drab street in Muide (Belgium).**

# *Introductory note*

This report presents the consolidated findings of a multi-national research study on *Coping with Social and Economic Change at Neighbourhood Level.* Established by the European Foundation for the Improvement of Living and Working Conditions, the study took place from 1987 to 1991. It investigated the role and contribution of local community action in responding to social and economic problems. The focus was on disadvantaged urban areas, and on the links between the actions of households, groups and organisations and policy makers in the public, private and voluntary sectors.

The methods of the research included an extensive review of literature and intensive case studies of residents' problems, local groups' activities and policy-makers' views in a large comparable locality in seven member states: Belgium, Greece, Ireland, the Netherlands, Portugal, Spain and the United Kingdom.

The report is in six chapters. The first provides a general orientation to the subject, background to the research process, key questions addressed, definition of key terms, and concludes with a description of each of the seven case-study localities, regarding physical, social and economic characteristics.

The second chapter gives the results of a survey of households in a selected neighbourhood which assembled information on residents' problems, where they looked to for help, how active they were on local issues and whether they made use of, or were involved in, local community groups.

The central part of the report, chapters three and four, analyses what local groups in the seven localities did and how they worked. It first outlines the nature of the whole local groups sector in each locality, then uses illustrations from case study groups, to show common and disparate factors. It proceeds to a discussion of how groups functioned, what resources they used and the special role of 'umbrella' groups.

Chapter five examines policies concerning local community action and relates them to the foregoing. Drawing on interviews with policy-makers at various levels, it shows how far the role of local groups was valued and supported, and to what extent partnership between authorities and local community groups was a reality.

The final chapter identifies key themes and conclusions from the study, relates them to the concerns of public policy, and presents recommendations for consideration by policy-makers at all levels.

**Creativity looking for better channels: open sewer in Oliveira do Douro (Portugal).**

**Development through self-reliance: women at the Archway project learn self-defence (Thamesmead, UK).**

# *Executive summary*

This research has examined how local community action relates to social policy in EC countries. It shows how people at neighbourhood level in disadvantaged urban areas are coping with social and economic change. It focuses on what local inhabitants do actively to solve their own problems, both independently and in partnership with authorities and other actors, and it draws conclusions for social cohesion and new forms of social policy.

## Background

It has long been recognised in the EC that economic advantage and disadvantage are to a large degree spatially concentrated. This applies not only at the macro level of countries and regions but at the micro level of cities, towns and neighbourhoods. The Single Market may further polarise economically advantaged and disadvantaged areas. In addition, there is intensified pressure on social services from demographic and social trends like increases in ageing, single parent families and homelessness.

**EC policy** addresses such imbalances in various ways, in partnership with national, regional and local government, at macro level by the Structural Funds, and at micro level by a variety of innovative social programmes. Such programmes, both by the EC and by national governments, stress the importance of involving local inhabitants actively in projects and partnerships to overcome disadvantage. However, it remains unclear what 'involving the local inhabitants' means in practical terms. The present research fills this gap, examining local community action in seven urban localities across the European Community, against the background of many other recent studies.

## The research

Started in 1987, this is a major investigation of social change and local action in **the Netherlands, Belgium, Ireland, the UK, Spain, Portugal and Greece.** Background information was also drawn from Italy, Germany and France. Implications of the report are the subject of analysis at a conference in Dublin in September 1992.

A wide review of existing sources about local community life was carried out, followed by a close look at a similar large disadvantaged locality in the seven countries. Researchers looked at the daily problems of people living in peripheral urban areas and how they tackled them, at how local groups and organisations worked, and at the views of policy-makers whose responsibilities affected that locality.

## The findings

People in all the localities used personal networks of family, friends and neighbours to help them with a range of problems. They had recourse to authorities for help with more official matters, and to a lesser extent used influential individuals and local community groups to help solve their problems. Groups were used more widely for general social purposes.

When respondents were asked how **satisfied** they were with the help they got from these sources there was a remarkably similar pattern. Satisfaction with personal networks was high, with authorities was low, with influential individuals was moderate and with local groups was high.

Despite different national voluntary sector traditions, every locality had a wide range of active local groups. These fell broadly into three types, or variations of them:

- **autonomous local community groups**, directly controlled by residents;
- **externally-led initiatives**, such as projects set up by the local authority or run by national voluntary organisations, churches, trade unions or mutual aid societies;
- **semi-autonomous groups**, being partnerships between residents and official agencies or other external bodies.

These groups were the main vehicles for participation in the public affairs of the locality. Small numbers of people played a central part, others helped or merely used the groups. About half the people in most localities used the groups to meet some part of their social needs, from recreation, sport and religion to tackling key issues in the locality like health, education, employment and amenities, or as vehicles to challenge, influence or support the public authorities.

There were important limitations to what groups could do: they did not usually reach the whole population; their role was often not widely understood; and they were often held back by lack of funding or policy support. Many groups were too small to reach all those in need of their services, were working on a 'shoestring' budget and were not widely known. In aggregate the groups were playing a crucial role in the life and development of the whole locality.

There were widespread similarities in the way many of the groups worked, the kinds of issues they tackled and the difficulties they faced. Every locality had an identifiable sector of local groups in the sense that there were networks of co-operation, local umbrella bodies and some official policies towards local groups which distinguished it from official public bodies, commercial businesses or individual households. In many cases groups helped each other, sometimes started other groups, ran joint campaigns, and generated information and experience. In other cases groups were more isolated.

Few governments, public authorities or national voluntary organisations had any strategy towards the local community action sector as a whole. Nearly all policies were short-term and piecemeal, and directed to particular organisations or projects. Similarly, community development bodies, where they existed, concentrated on a limited selection of groups.

Since policy lays such stress on mobilising the input of local people to help solve the problems of disadvantaged localities, it was important to examine to what extent the input at local level was from residents themselves or from outside bodies. People in the groups were asked 'who runs your organisation - who decides what really happens?' and questions were posed about resources and volunteering.

In six of the seven countries a majority of local groups were autonomous. The next largest number were semi-autonomous, and slightly fewer were those that were externally controlled. The majority of groups were unique to their locality; some worked across adjoining localities; a minority were members of national organisations.

## Conclusions

Conclusions about local community action included the following:

- Local inhabitants in disadvantaged urban areas are **continually involved in activity to cope with and improve their situation**. Much of this activity takes place in **households**, through **personal networks** and through **dealing with the authorities**. In its most sustained and concentrated form it takes place through **groups and organisations.**

- Local community action largely **springs from the need of local inhabitants to solve joint problems of daily living.** Much local activity springs from needs such as **caring** for children, old people and people with disabilities, **improving local amenities** and **providing local activities.** In economic convention, these areas of unpaid but intensive work are **concealed behind the phrase 'economic inactivity'.**

- Most local groups and organisations are **created by the residents themselves**, others by public authorities or national voluntary organisations. There is a **permanent local groups sector**, playing a **long-term role in local development**, whilst the interventions of authorities at this level are usually in the form of short-term projects.

- Most funding and access to policy goes to a small circle of organisations treated by the authorities as satellites for **extending service delivery.**

- The longer-lived independent local organisations have a **long-term view of the interests of the locality**, and pressure the authorities to **carry out or maintain development.**

- There is more similarity at the local level than would be guessed from apparent differences in the nature of national voluntary sectors in the different countries. Local community action is the **common ground of voluntary action across different countries**, albeit with distinct national and regional characteristics.

- Local community action is a **vital component in European development** but its nature is little understood and its potential only partially realised. There is a need for **strategies at all levels** to ensure that local community action can flourish as a **permanent aspect of social and economic development.** Principles for such strategies and recommendations for social policy are presented at the end of the report.

# Chapter one
# What is local community action?

## Introduction

### Fundamental yet hidden

*'Involving local inhabitants in the improvement of deprived areas'; 'Increasing the participation of residents'; 'Intervening in neighbourhoods in crisis'; 'Increasing the role of the voluntary sector in the delivery of social services'; 'Building local partnerships to overcome disadvantage'.*

What do these phrases mean? Why have they become an increasing part of social debate and policy in the countries of Europe?

In 1987 the European Foundation began a study to test out these ideas against concrete realities. It looks at how neighbourhoods and localities work. It looks before and beyond the process of 'intervention' to ask what it is that is being intervened *in*. It asks what is meant by 'participation': can the whole of a local population participate in decision-making about the locality?

New social policy often stresses the need to 'involve local inhabitants'. But does this mean merely drawing them into activities provided and directed by authorities? How is it related to initiatives taken by the residents themselves? Does it mean a real partnership in the sense of shared initiative, shared resources and shared control?

Conventional social analysis recognises only a 'macro' and 'micro' world. It speaks of society and the individual, the state and the household. But between the micro and the macro lies the semi-public, semi-private space of the locality. Here all sorts of transactions take place that hold society together, that form the links between individuals and society. Here are the larger or smaller networks of friends, families, neighbours which form people's social context; here are the amenities or the lack of amenities which make daily life easier or harder; here are the voluntary organisations, pressure groups, shared activities, innovative projects which transform a turbulent mass of private concerns into public issues. This is the area that needs to be studied if we are to see what the involvement of local inhabitants really means.

## Origins of the research

In recent years public policies at both the European and national levels have looked increasingly towards the sphere of local citizen activity for responses to social and economic problems - in health, employment, crime, environment, poverty, race relations and many other areas. The need for a clearer understanding of the nature and potential of local life is underlined by the advent of the Single European Market. Recent socio-economic analyses have pointed to changes which threaten the quality of life of individuals, families and communities in certain areas. Previous work of the European Foundation (for example by Burton, Forest and Stewart, 1987) analysed the emerging patterns of economic change and social polarisation. Whilst economic changes were improving prosperity for many, they were increasing disadvantage for others. The pace of European development seemed to threaten a widening gap between those geographical areas and localities which could benefit most easily from deregulated trade and those which stood to lose out because of such factors as the collapse of traditional forms of industry or the underdevelopment of modern communications infrastructure.

Economic pressures have also coincided with a widespread sense of crisis in public services. Where substantial public services are in operation there are many indications that they have become cumbersome. At the same time, increasing proportions of unemployed people and others in need such as single-parent families and the homeless, are putting strain on the capacity of the services. Where public services have not been adequately developed, particularly in some of the southern countries, there is a dilemma about how to develop them without generating undue bureaucracy and overdependence. Throughout the European Community the costs of public services are rising due to increased demand, and there is pressure to reduce public budgets and seek cheaper, more efficient solutions in order to stabilise the economy. All this lends added urgency to the sense that solutions must include better targeting and integration of services at the local level. This includes increasing emphasis on the role and contribution of local citizen action.

## The focus of innovation

Since the signing of the Single European Act, the EC has been increasingly concerned to deliver its commitment to social cohesion as well as economic development. It is addressing regional imbalances and local problems by means of the Structural Funds and a wide range of social action programmes. In these measures, and in many more mounted by individual member states, policy-makers invoke the importance of remedial action being targeted at the local level and actively involving different local interests. An integrated local approach is pursued mainly in programmes to assist economic development and to combat unemployment and poverty.

Many of the new approaches are based on a notion of 'integration' or 'partnership' between different public, private and voluntary agencies. In EC measures, wider social issues have generally been subsumed under the area of economic development; but the experience of the innovative programmes, action research and information exchanges frequently points to the connections between economic problems and other social and political factors. For example the principles of 'solidarity' and 'partnership' adopted by the third Poverty Programme, now in progress, were based on conclusions from evaluation of a network of exploratory local projects across Europe: 'The central element in adequate action lies in curbing and transcending the processes which create dependence and increase the impotence of communities and individuals, through greater support for the social, economic and cultural self-determination of those concerned, especially by means of associative development which, in various forms, reinstates them as citizens and interlocutors vis a vis the services and their environment' (Hiernaux, 1989).

With the adoption of the Social Charter and an explicit concern with 'living conditions' at the Maastricht summit in late 1991, the stage was set for a more integrated and balanced approach to social and economic conditions. While current programmes have increasingly invoked local participation as an indispensible ingredient, few have stood back **to examine the nature of local community action itself.** In the complexity of partnerships involving local authorities, private businesses, various institutions and national and European projects, the citizens' direct contribution tends to remain in the shadows. Clearly if such partnerships are to succeed, it is essential to draw out the residents' role; to understand its nature and see where its energy comes from; to examine what functions it already performs in the life of localities, who is part of it and who is left out; to identify what factors facilitate and hinder it; and to understand how it is affected by policies which seek to draw it into partnerships.

## A distinct sector

The research programme reported in these pages identifies a distinct field, **local community action**, which is different from the formal services of public institutions on the one hand and from the private life of individuals and households on the other. Local community action means *any collective, public or quasi-public effort involving the active unpaid participation of inhabitants which addresses the perceived needs of people living in that locality.*

For brevity this report often refers to this area simply as 'local action'. It should be clear from the context that this refers throughout primarily to the independent voluntary actions of citizens in their local communities, whether through their informal networks, through their own groups and organisations or through participation in forums or organisations created by others. Definitions of key terms used to describe this field are provided later in this chapter.

There are **three fundamental sources** of local community action:
- independent activity by local residents
- activity led by public authorities
- activity organised by other established bodies such as national voluntary organisations, industry, trade unions or the church.

The study examines the role played by each of these, their different characteristics, their relative contribution to local action and how they interact. It considers how the local community action sector as a whole contributes to **meeting people's needs**, especially in areas undergoing stressful social and economic change, and how it **relates to public policies**, whether of the EC, national governments or local authorities. Finally it proposes **strategies** about the role of this sector in relation to social and economic policies at many levels.

While the study does not claim to be comprehensive it is an exceptional body of information. It investigates the whole local action sector in a large, comparable locality in each of seven European countries; in each case it investigates three different perpectives on local action - groups and organisations, people in households, and a range of policy-makers; and for each country this is set against the whole national background on this issue. The findings throw a major new shaft of light onto social policy issues.

**Participation in local community action is more difficult if you do not have an adequate roof over your head: makeshift housing in Oliveira do Douro (Portugal).**

Before presenting these findings, which occupy the main body of the report, the remainder of this chapter describes **how the investigation was carried out**; explains more about the **context** of the research; provides a conceptual framework of **definitions** of key words used in the report; and gives a brief picture of the **seven localities** in which detailed fieldwork took place.

# How the investigation was carried out

The research was carried out between 1987 and 1991. With the original title *Coping with Social and Economic Change at Neighbourhood Level*, its aims were:
- to examine the importance of local life in contemporary European society;
- to determine factors which influence the ability of people in local communities to cope with and respond to their changing conditions;
- to examine how the ability to cope is affected by current social and economic policies; and
- to analyse the thinking about neighbourhood and local community life which underlies current policy development.

The research fell into three periods:
1. a wide-ranging review of literature and some exploratory interviews; this phase was carried out in four countries, **Belgium, the Netherlands, Ireland and the United Kingdom**;
2. collation and interpretation of the evidence from the four countries in a **bibliography** (Boucneau, Decleir et al, 1989) and an **interim consolidated report** (Chanan and Vos, 1989); plus the establishment of a common method for fieldwork analysis, and the involvement of a further three countries, **Portugual, Spain and Greece**;
3. the **fieldwork phase** in all seven countries, collection of background evidence from several more, and interpretation and comparison of the findings.

Phases one and two of the research are presented in separate publications and therefore will not be fully described here. The main sources are the four initial national reports (from Netherlands, Belgium, Ireland and the UK), the bibliography and first consolidated report mentioned above, and the *Research Plan* for the fieldwork phase (Ronayne, Duggan et al, 1989). The key concepts and findings emerging from these are integral to the way the fieldwork was approached and so to the findings and discussion in this concluding report.

The first and second stages of the study, which included the development of international dialogue amongst the researchers, established that in order to understand local community action it was important to look at **fairly large localities**, not just small neighbourhoods in isolation. Neighbourhoods in the sense of a few close streets are foci for many aspects of social life but do not amount to self-sufficient systems either administratively or in terms of human relations. Boundaries are subjective, varying according to the individual and household, and many personal and group networks flow across them. However, within large localities, distinct neighbourhoods can often be seen.

A single major case study of a large and comparable locality was done in each country. From the earlier phases of the research there was extensive second-hand information on interventions at local community level over the past generation. The key problem which now needed tackling was **how to get an 'inside' picture of local community action**. This demanded intensive work using several different sources including, crucially, direct household interviewing. This needed to be paralleled by a survey of the whole of the relevant local action sector and an even closer look at some of the key organisations. This 'triangular' approach was completed by interviewing a range of policy-makers at different levels affecting the services of the locality.

The limitation of having only one case study in each country was ameliorated by two factors: firstly maintaining the collection of second-hand information from other studies and contemporaneous national developments; secondly by ensuring a high degree of comparability in the research method used in each country.

The latter was achieved by the detailed design of the study. Localities were chosen which had certain similar characteristics, namely being fairly **large** (not less than 12,500 people, average about 30,000); having an **identity and boundary** that was generally acknowledged and related to administrative structures; being **peripheral to a major economic centre**; having higher than average indicators of **social problems and needs**; and having some evidence of **active local community responses** to those problems.

Each locality was studied in the same way. Five **priority social issues** were established as being of particular interest on the basis of their importance to European and national policy and in current social debate: **unemployment; health; education and training; the environment, including built environment; and transport.** The position of **women** in local action was a further topic of special attention. These priority themes informed the importance to be attached to local groups, the dialogue with policy-makers, and the interpretation of residents' concerns.

A **household questionnaire** was administered to a random selection of the adult population in a selected neighbourhood or part of the locality. The core of this questionnaire was identical for all seven localities, only allowing for nuances of translation and culture. Residents were asked open questions about how they saw the locality and its problems, what kinds of action they took in dealing with them; and then whether they knew of, used or participated in local groups. These open responses were then complemented by a series of specific questions.

In parallel, lists were made of **all the local action groups** involving voluntary participation that could be found operating in the locality, whether originated by residents, authorities or other agencies. Analysis was then focussed on those which appeared to be addressing one or more of the priority issues. The groups were then surveyed to establish their activities, methods of operation, resources and who was involved in them centrally and peripherally, and four or five in each locality were studied intensively regarding their entire operation, role and effects. Three core questioins underlay the analysis of the significance of the groups:
1 Why and how do people use local groups and organisations in coping with problems?
2 How do local groups and organisations deal with social, economic, environmental or other issues which arise in the locality where they operate? and
3 What role do policy-makers see for local organisations in dealing with problems and issues which are experienced in the locality?

The three sides of the fieldwork triangle - **residents' views, local groups, and public policies towards local action** - form in turn the basis for the central chapters of the report. Most of the detailed material and illustration is taken from the seven national reports. Direct quotations from these are referred to throughout by the page number in the English editions and by a single letter referring to the nationality of the report, as follows:
    B: Belgium
    G: Greece
    I: Ireland
    N: Netherlands
    P: Portugal
    S: Spain
    U: United Kingdom.
The full references for these reports will be found at the beginning of the reference section.

# The context for local action

## More detailed questions

In the literature on local area development there is always a great readiness to claim the involvement of local inhabitants. This is now virtually a mark of authenticity, an indication of working to a model of long-term independence rather than increased dependence; but this involvement is not often demonstrated in a visible way. There is rarely a detached look at

A meeting of the Unemployed Shipyard Workers' group consider changes in welfare benefits. Their voluntary workshop makes products for social use at home and abroad (Amsterdam Mid-North, the Netherlands).

the condition of the local community before and after intervention. There is rarely any audit of the pre-existing signs of independent activity, of which autonomous groups are the clearest, of their condition, their aims and the difficulties they face. The role of inhabitants usually remains a shadowy background.

In many cases there is not even any mention in local development studies of groups and organisations, only of 'the local population' as an amorphous mass, or supposedly typified in a small number of individuals. Given the low profile, low status and low resources of local groups, it is easy to ignore them in official or external views of an area. But it is quite clear that to do so is to ignore the primary evidence of the indigenous life of the inhabitants, and to ignore the most authentic *prima facie* vehicle for the expression of their views and wishes.

Within the general questions raised above it will be valuable to distinguish more detailed aspects which are often blurred together. For example, to what extent is it justifiable to speak of a **local community action *sector*?** Is it just a collection of unconnected groups? Can one generalise about this across all countries or does it have to be described quite differently from country to country? If such a sector does exist, to what extent does it represent local people? If it reaches only half the populaton can it be regarded as representative? How crucial is the existence of such a sector to life and development in the locality?

Concerning the role of local action in relation to **public services**, several questions may be distinguished:
- does local action provide **substitute** public services?
- does it **increase the efficiency** of public services?
- does it **reduce dependency** on public services?
- does it increase people's long-term capacity to **meet their own needs**?
- does it reach **the most deprived**?
- does it increase people's ability to **participate** in democratic processes?

Similarly, concerning how it **functions**:
- who makes it happen?
- how does it work?
- what stops it from happening?
- what conditions does it need in order to flourish?

Some of the key evidence needed in order to answer these questions lies in the **close study of local groups** and their relation to external factors. It lies in information on:
- active members, other members, users and other beneficiaries;
- use of volunteers and paid workers;
- relevance of the groups to public policy issues;
- functioning and resourcing of the groups;
- balance of input from local residents, from the authorities and from external sources;
- how the various inputs interact both within and between specific local organisations.

## Intervention and the permanent partner

What is new about studying local community action? Do not governments, local authorities and national voluntary or charitable bodies already know how it all works? Surprisingly, perhaps, local action is often assumed or invoked as a background factor, but rarely examined in its own right. Each relevant body has a partial view. Practices in this area tend to be piecemeal, and policies rely on untested assumptions. No one of the major actors in this field has a comprehensive approach to local action or examines its fundamental nature.

Public policy has always acknowledged that regions, areas and localities display very different characters and conditions. There are rich and poor areas, industrial and rural areas, administrative and suburban areas. The EC, national governments and local authorities respond to statistics on economic, demographic and social trends, but these do not reveal the inner life of the locality, its informal networks and its self-created organisations. Innovative programmes are an important part of the context for this study, but they constitute only one segment of local action. In order to understand how they work it is necessary to examine the larger hidden context of **continuous action** by local people.

## Importance of autonomy

Current notions of citizen action are often unclear as to where they mean:
a  people doing things **for others**,
b  people doing things **for themselves**, and
c  people **supporting state provision**.
All three are important but it cannot be seen what role each should play until their different inputs into local action can be discerned.

Whilst there is general agreement in theory that people should be 'helped to help themselves', in practice there is widespread confusion as between forms of helping which help people with an acute need and those which help them in a way that increases their long term independence.

If one of the aims of policy is to increase people's capacity to meet their own needs, it is important to be able to see where an activity is **primarily driven by local people themselves** and where it is **provided by the authorities or by other external input**. Are the different elements mixing well, enhancing each other, or are they pulling in opposite directions? This question is discussed more fully in chapters three and four.

# The interface with public authorities

The boundaries of local community action are rarely clear; in particular, does it include action by public authorities?

For present purposes it may be anticipated that most of the actions of public and local authorities are not in themselves local community action because they are not carried out by citizens under their independent initiative but take place within a prescribed legal framework. Local authorities in most countries derive at least part of their authority and their obligations from the state rather than just from the local electorate. It is true that there are many variations; small municipalities, in particular, may be more wholly accountable to local people. This is the case, for example, in Greece and Portugal, where these lowest tiers of public authority do have a similar character to local citizen initiatives. In France there is a dual system whereby the state exercises its regional and local authority through its officials, the Prefects, but certain areas of policy and provision, such as recreation and primary schools, are in the hands of small municipalities which are wholly accountable to the local electorate and are not seen as part of the state apparatus.

In these cases one might include municipalities in 'local action'; more often, the local authorities, even though elected by local citizens, are in practice largely controlled by the state or region. They are usually staffed by professionals and operate as large corporations. In many localities they are among the largest or are actually the largest employer. Outside their main programmes **local authorities are often major partners** in the creation or facilitation of new local action. By entering into partnerships with other local organisations they may engender semi-autonomous initiatives which merge into the local action sector.

Whatever their power-base, the role of public and local authorities in *responding to* and *supporting* local action is crucial. This is illustrated both positively and negatively in the research findings. The current concern to 'involve the inhabitant' is one of the main stimuli to the present research, and by looking more objectively at the **three key points** of the local triangle - people in their households, local action groups and authorities' policies and attitudes - this study aims to contribute to establishing how the interaction of these components can be maximised.

# Definitions

It remains, before presenting the findings, to provide a guide to the definition of key terms used in this report. It is not possible in this neglected field to appeal to well-established and universal definitions. Language in this area is often unclear. In addition there are many different national variations of emphasis and experience. It was an important part of the

# Table 1.1: Defining local community action

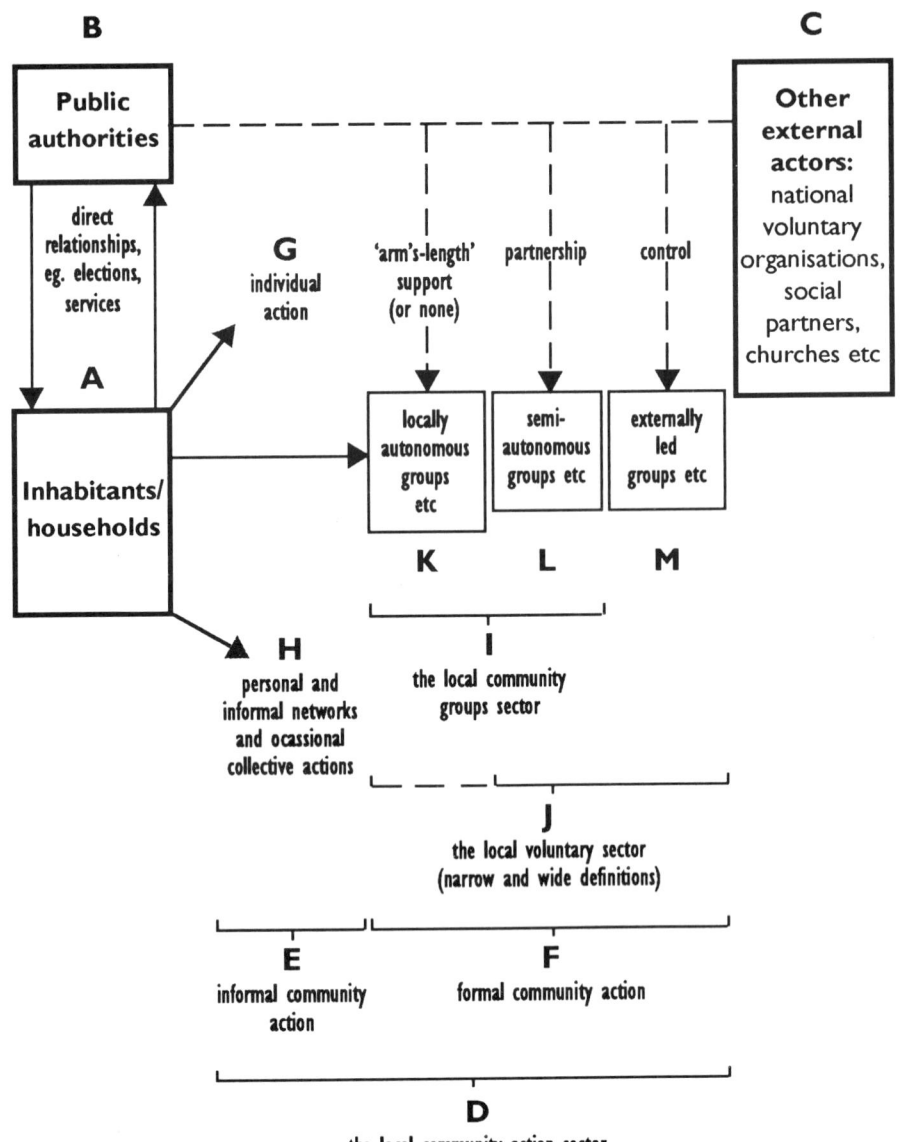

international research dialogue to achieve a common understanding of the phenomena being studied, and thus to establish a **framework of key terms** that could be applied in all countries. The following definitions are therefore, in the first place, a **guide to the usage** that has been adopted in this report; secondly they are in themselves a product of the research, and as such are recommended as helpful in **mapping this field and informing policies.**

The main areas are illustrated in **Table 1.1**. The broadest categories are at the bottom of the diagram, working upwards to the more detailed distinctions.

Inevitably, diagrams and definitions tend to oversimplify the phenomena, and it must be stressed that the key terms represent essences rather than firm boundaries. Additionally, to explain the definitions requires some anticipation of findings.

Some areas remain stubbornly ambiguous. This is not just an attribute of the language used but of the phenomena being represented. In the definitions, therefore, attention is drawn to certain **crucial ambiguities** which indicate important dilemmas in interpreting this field, and which are therefore the subject of fuller analysis later in the report.

The key actors who **create** this field are:
- **local inhabitants** (point A in the diagram)
- **public authorities** (point B) and
- **other external actors** (C) such as national voluntary organisations, the commercial sector, churches and trade unions.

The field of concern in this research, the **local community action sector** (D), is seen as distinct from, and taking place outside, the central functions of the three main types of actor. Thus the sector does not include the private life of local inhabitants in their households (A); it does not include the centralised or routine responsibilities of the public authorities (B); it does not include the national offices and actions of the voluntary organisations, trade unions, political parties or churches (C). Nor does it include commercial activity and paid work, except insofar as there may be paid staff or trading activity incorporated into local groups or initiatives; or insofar as private companies may participate in partnerships or support local organisations, in which case they feature among the 'other external actors' (C).

Local community action may of course be *concerned* with all these, and more particularly with their impact at local level.

It is arguable that actions **within households** should also qualify as local community action. Indeed, it may be held that they are the basic components of such action. The research emphatically recognises the importance of actions and interactions which take place within households. It was decided, however, that a clearer picture, and a better reflection of common usage, could be obtained by regarding these as being outside the sphere of local community action as such. Local community action is limited to

*13*

actions which have some degree of visible **public** presence or significance. Maintaining this boundary enables us to pose the crucial question: what is the *relationship* between local community action and the private life of inhabitants? The household, however, is not to be understood as a physical boundary: a neighbourhood meeting can be held in a private house, and many a local group has been administered from a cardboard box kept under somebody's bed.

Local community action, then, includes all **unpaid, self-motivated activity by inhabitants which expresses or impinges on the shared life or conditions of the inhabitants** in the locality; it may also include **action taken by authorities or other actors which mobilises or involves such action by inhabitants**. It does not include action by authorities or other actors *towards* local inhabitants which does not actively involve them.

The relevant actions of inhabitants can include **individual action** (G), such as taking up an issue about local conditions with the authorities; **informal joint action** (H), such as participating in a network of friends, relatives or neighbours in order to provide mutual assistance or carry out activities; **occasional collective action** (H again) such as one-off meetings and demonstrations; and participation in all kinds of **local groups, organisations and initiatives** (K,L,M).

These different types of action may of course flow into one another, and the *degree* to which they exemplify local community action may vary from weak to strong: a group which sustains an explicit concern over months or years is of course a more intensive form of local community action than an occasional individual complaint. Hence the more organised and sustained forms of action - defined here as **formal community action** (F) are highly significant for this field, and this research pays special attention to them; but the aggregate of **informal community action** (E) is no less important.

Further distinctions can now be made, particularly within the formal part. The key distinctions to be made concern **the degree to which a body is carrying out the actions of local inhabitants** as distinct from other actors. This is primarily to do with who controls the actions of the body. Providers of resources often attach conditions to their allocation, and hence acquire a degree of control. This remains an ambiguous area. Some resources, especially official funding, carry much weight in formal definitions of the functions of a group, whilst others, especially the voluntary labour of participants, may not. This obscures the real resource-profile, and even self-concept, of local organisations, making it difficult to assess how autonomous they are. Additionally, this is an area where national traditions and terminology vary widely. In Belgium, for example, local action groups are usually run by paid professionals and are called 'private organisations'. These would not be seen as part of the voluntary sector, a term reserved for charitable groups usually connected with the church.

Accepting these uncertain boundaries, it is nevertheless possible to categorise groups broadly into those whose programme is mainly determined by residents, and which can therefore be called **locally autonomous** (K); those whose programme is determined by outside bodies, which are called **externally-led** (M), and those jointly determined by residents and outside bodies, the **semi-autonomous** (L).

The jointly-controlled programmes are therefore one form of **partnership** between local residents and other actors; but it is vital to note that there may be other kinds of partnership which either do not aim for or do not achieve a significant role for local residents in joint direction of the action. For example many local partnership arrangements are partnerships *between different official agencies* or *between official agencies and other external partners*, with little or no participative role ascribed to local inhabitants. In these cases the initiatives are in reality externally-led (M). For a group or initiative to be a partnership in the sense of this research, there must be some real element of decision-making by local inhabitants.

One final ambiguity is crucial to the present exercise, namely the definition of the voluntary sector, more particularly **the local voluntary sector** (J). Differences in national tradition and even legal definition make this an area where systematic terminology cannot be imposed. Comparison of national voluntary sectors across the countries of the EC is only now being begun (see Harvey, 1992). Particularly significant for the present exercise are variations in the relationships between national and local bodies. In some countries, such as the UK, the term 'voluntary sector' is used loosely to cover all forms of non-statutory body, from large, professionally-run national organisations down to small and entirely independent community groups with no paid staff. Along with this usage goes an assumption (not borne out by this study) that the national bodies in some way control or represent the aggregate of local bodies. In some other countries 'the voluntary sector' is generally regarded as meaning only national organisations and their constituent local branches, if any, whilst independent local bodies are called associations. In yet other countries the number of national voluntary or charitable organisations is small and they are not generally thought of as a 'sector'. In any of these cases, there may be further diversity in practice between national bodies which establish and control local branches from the centre, and national bodies which represent or provide a service for a network of local organisations which are fundamentally independent.

It was beyond the scope of this research to dissect all these variations, but it was necessary to adopt a language which could both reflect the importance of the national-local relationship, wherever it existed, and indicate its limitations. Since the commonest understanding of '**local voluntary sector**' was that of organisations with a formal link to national or regional (or occasionally international) charitable or benevolent bodies, it was reasonable to adopt this usage (J, narrow definition). Such local bodies are therefore mainly found either amongst the externally-led (M) or the semi-autonomous (L).

Conversely, where it is necessary to refer to all groups which are locally-controlled, either wholly or in part, the appropriate term is the **local community groups sector** (I). The fact that this overlaps with the local voluntary sector (narrow definition) at point L correctly expresses the uncertainty often found in practice as to where the boundary of the local voluntary sector should be drawn on the continuum with the less formalised group activities of local citizens.

Two further qualifications must be made about the narrow definition of 'the local voluntary sector'. Firstly, examples can also be found of **local bodies which are highly developed as formal voluntary organisations**, yet which remain firmly under the control of local residents. Such cases would clearly be included in any description of the local voluntary sector. Secondly, wherever 'local voluntary sector' is used to indicate **all groups which provide a vehicle for volunteering**, locally autonomous groups must also be included. In this case, the wider definition must be adopted, and the 'local voluntary sector' (J, wider definition) becomes synonymous with formal community action (F). In the remainder of this report, however, the narrow definition is employed unless otherwise stated.

# The case study localities

The following short descriptions are intended to convey some of the character of the research fieldwork areas. Detailed statistical, historical and other information is contained in the national reports. These descriptions refer to 1990, when the fieldwork was carried out.

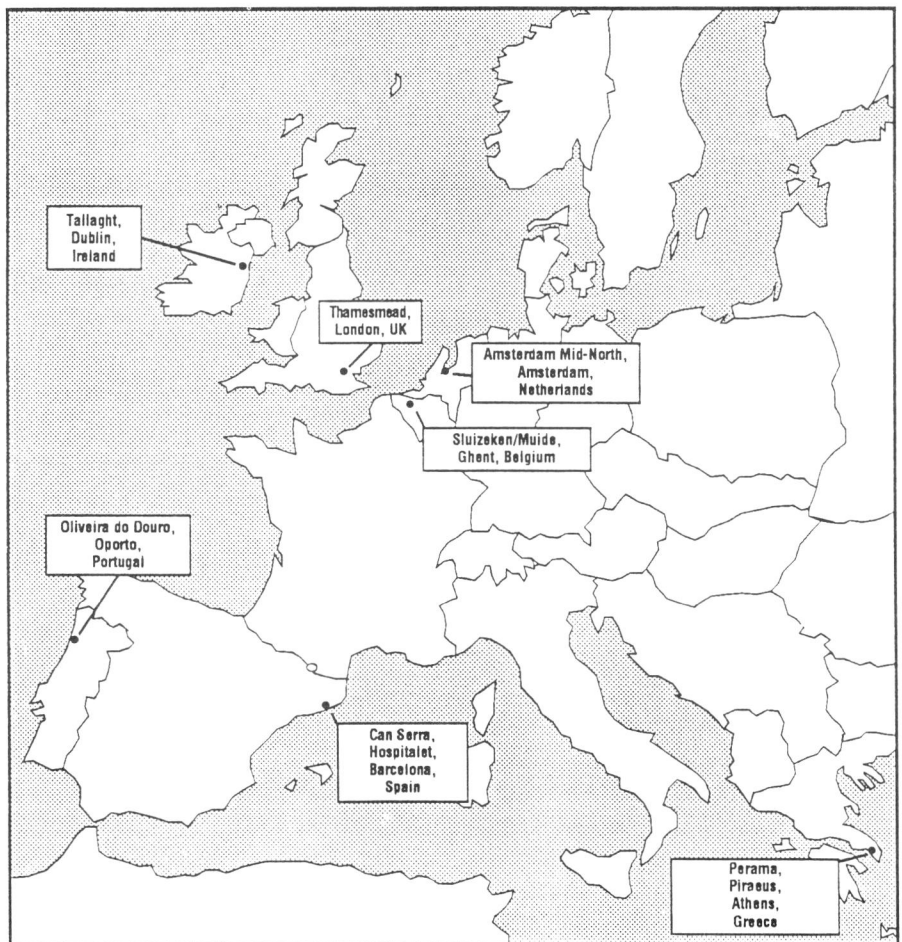

# Sluizeken and Muide, Ghent, Belgium

Ghent, a city of 232,000 inhabitants, is the capital of East Flanders. In the 19th century, Ghent underwent rapid growth based on the port and the linen and cotton industries. The population almost doubled between 1801 and 1846, from 55,000 to 103,000. From 1860 the clearance of crowded inner city areas drove many residents to the industrialised outer areas which in turn became built up into living areas now known as the '19th century Ghent belt'. The 'belt' consists of seven neighbourhoods typified by an accumulation of problems imposed by social and economic changes over a period of a century. A quarter of the population of the modern city, 55,000 people, live in this 4% of its geographical area. Sluizeken and Muide are two of these neighbourhoods, adjoining each other on the northern edge of the inner city, close to the port.

Between 1970 and 1988 the resident population of Ghent decreased by 18% as better-off young people people moved out to surrounding districts, leaving some city areas populated disproportionately by people in poorer conditions. At the same time there was an increase in commuting, the city remaining an economic centre. But prosperity among the city residents has been declining since 1970, as de-urbanisation has led to the relative increase in the proportion of less well-off groups such as the elderly, the unemployed and migrants. There is a substantial community of Turkish origin. In the 19th century Ghent belt 37% of the population are unskilled, having had only primary education, and 46% of the housing is in poor or moderately poor condition. The unemployment rate in the Ghent belt is about 33% as against 10% in the city as a whole.

Sluizeken and Muide have been dependent on the docks industry for their ups and downs. Businesses and population grew in Sluizeken during the 18th and 19th centuries. Then the harbour was extended northwards, Muide grew and Sluizeken declined. The new and flourishing centre of commerce suffered in its turn, with a further northward move of the docks industry and the opening of a better connecting road between the centre and the port.

Sluizeken still has a larger population - 7,500 to Muide's 5,000. Since 1974 Sluizeken has become home to a large number of immigrants, forming about 27% of the population there in 1981. Most are Turkish and come from the same rural district of Emirdag. Their population structure is young compared with the indigenous population which in this neighbourhood is rather elderly, with a considerable number of retired seamen and unemployed. Muide is also more isolated, situated between the docks, railway and Muide bridge. When the bridge is open for shipping and the railway crossings closed, the neighbourhood is inaccessible.

Problems in both neighbourhoods include housing, traffic, education, unemployment, low incomes and poor health. Traffic is heavy on the through routes, and there are few parks or playgrounds. Houses are decaying or overcrowded and many do not have adequate sanitary facilities.

In 1983 parts of the Ghent belt were earmarked for improvement under a new government urban renewal initiative, based on partnership between the various relevant authorities, which stipulated resident involvement. But the process was cumbersome and underfinanaced, and little change had taken place by 1989. In that year a new political authority assumed power in Ghent, and following several years' pressure from residents' organisations, began to take more decisive measures. A tax on empty houses is to be used to finance renovation projects, and the Ghent belt has been designated an area of housing shortage, enabling it to qualify for considerable government aid. There is also benefit from the 'Lenssens' fund, an anti-poverty drive under the Flemish minister for family and welfare. Ghent has received approval for five projects, on: 1. building work for the long-term unemployed; 2. intercultural co-operation and youth work amongst migrants; 3. basic education and literacy for the unskilled; 4. emergency reception centres for women and children under stress; and 5. planning of permanent co-ordinating agencies to integrate welfare and community work in each underprivileged neighbourhood. These are in early stages of implementation.

# Perama, Piraeus, Athens, Greece

Perama is a municipality on the south-western edge of the Athens conurbation. Its natural limits are the foothills of the Aigaleos Oros to the north, and the sea to the south. The town extends along a narrow coastal strip which is terminated at the western end by the naval dockyard installations, while at the eastern end it is joined to the rest of the Athens basin via a single access road.

Perama, with a population of 30,000, is the youngest municipality in the district of Piraeus. The residential area dates from the 1920's. Settlement took place largely by creeping encroachments on land belonging to the Organisation for

the Management of Church Estates (ODEP). The town developed especially during the 'fifties, when its population trebled. A town plan was instituted in 1960 but encroachments continued into the eastern part of the area, occupied by fuel installations, causing clashes with the authorities. In 1985 the town plan was extended along the shore below the railway lines, and a process was begun whereby ODEP ceded land to the government so that growth could be properly planned. Delay in the completion of this process has held up investment in the necessary infrastructure. Water supply and sewerage are poor, with some houses in the marginal areas still having no running water and having to collect water from municipal standpipes.

The percentage of manual workers in Perama, at 62%, is the highest in the Athens basin. Most local employment is connected with the shipbuilding and repair yards, which are subject to seasonal fluctuations. These are not reflected in the official unemployment figure, about 5%, which also conceals the fact that only 13% of women of working age are employed - extremely low compared even with the generally low rate of 23% for Athens as a whole. This is connected with the fact that the shipbuilding and repair industry traditionally does not employ women, while poor transport connections with the rest of the Athens basin make commuting extremely difficult. There is a good deal of unrecorded pieceworking done at home by women in the area, and also by children, for such industries as clothing, toys and nets. The proportion of children in the locality is high, and that of old people relatively low.

The level of education is low but improving. Illiteracy was considerably reduced in the 1970s but is still double the average for Greater Athens. The failure rate in secondary education is high, and not many students go on to succeed in further and higher education.

Pollution and environmental hazards are a particular problem in Perama. Storage tanks containing petroleum products create fumes and a risk of explosions. Explosives are regularly transported to the islands from the port of Hercules. There are fumes from a landfill site used for dumping rubbish, and the central sewage outfall discharges into the sea between Perama and Keratsinion - a problem awaiting the completion of a waste-processing plant at Psittalia.

Transport is poor, and the inadequacy of the single road into the locality was a subject of mass demonstrations by local residents in 1988 and 89. Social facilities and recreation areas are inadequate, and it is difficult to find suitable spaces for the creation of better ones, owing to the density of the existing built-up areas and the fact that most of the remainder of the municipality belongs to ODEP, the Piraeus Port Authority, the Naval dockyard or industrial companies. Local people and the Municipal administration itself have fought with some success to draw attention to the problems of the area and secure help from the landowners and the government. An area has been allocated for a marine sports centre, and another for the establishment of a technical college.

The powers of municipalities have been extended since 1985, so that they can in theory take action on most issues affecting the locality, but this is not backed up by decentralisation of budgets. A Local Development Programme was adopted in 1988 but with no guarantee of central funds its implementation is uncertain. However, Perama was selected as a site for the EC's third Poverty Programme, bringing an injection of resources, which have given a boost to various local improvement initiatives.

# Tallaght, Dublin, Ireland

Tallaght is a large 'satellite' town built up rapidly during the '60s and '70s around an older village situated to the south west of the city of Dublin. In this period Dublin was experiencing rapid population growth due to increased urbanisation and a fall in emigration: an increase from 663,000 to 915,000 between 1960 and 1980. At the same time there was a process of inner city decline and a shift in residence to the suburbs, particularly to three 'new towns', of which Tallaght is the largest.

In the '80s there was also a major fall in industrial employment in Dublin, while employment in services remained static. There was therefore a large increase in unemployment: in the Greater Dublin area it increased from 5% to 18% between 1971 and 1988. There was a slight improvement towards the end of the decade, and the population also began to decrease again, due to a declining birth rate and renewed emigration. The proportion of women in employment has steadily risen, but many of these are in part-time and low-paid jobs, which have been increasing as a proportion of the total. These trends are accentuated in Tallaght, where unemployment stands at 23%, and in West Tallaght over 50%. Youth unemployment is a particular cause of concern.

Tallaght's intensive building programme, between 1970 and 1985, was accompanied by a phenomenal increase in population, from 6,000 to 69,000. The major influx was of young couples or families attracted by the new public housing and relatively cheap private housing opportunities. The growth has now stopped but the area has a very high proportion of children and young people. By 1981, 45 per cent of the population was under 15 compared with 30% for Ireland as a whole.

The town's growth was based on a government report of 1966 and a Dublin

County plan of 1972, but has not had a specific agency to coordinate it. Whilst many public and private agencies have been involved, the growth of facilities has been inadequate, and in particular has left the town ill-fitted to generate employment opportunities. Originally an industrial policy parallelled the growth in housing, but this was not sustained.

Development has mostly followed a model of relatively self-contained neighbourhoods each with its own commercial provision, but this pattern has not been fully realised. Several estates are severely under-provided for in terms of services and amenities. This has forced a reliance on central provision, itself not great, and led to problems of access and cost. The isolation of women rearing young children, often on their own, is a particular problem. Youth crime is rising.

Social amenities in Tallaght are variable. Most estates have churches, youth clubs, community centres and sports facilities, the latter more suitable for boys than girls. There is only one swimming pool. Many voluntary sports groups make use of the facilities but are often constrained by lack of resources. Shopping and commercial facilities are less well spread but a major new shopping centre has recently opened.

There are 32 primary schools in Tallaght and nine secondary schools. The rate of pupils leaving school without qualifications is double the national figure. There is a network of adult education provision including a special Vocational Training Opportunities Scheme which was piloted there and has now been extended throughout the country. An innovative voluntary sector pre-school programme for disadvantaged children is planned.

Tallaght has as yet no hospital of its own, though one is planned. Three health centres provide services, insufficient for the needs of the population, and partly made up by voluntary agencies. About 20% of households are totally dependent on social welfare payments. In West Tallaght the figure is over 40%. Many people find that information on entitlements and how to get them is inadequate.

The development of the road system is well advanced, and there are new plans for industrial development through upgrading an existing site into a high quality business park. A Regional Technical College is also planned. A new local authority is planned for Belgard County, in which Tallaght is situated, and should improve the capacity to coordinate developments.

Tallaght benefitted from the second European Poverty Programme by the establishment of the West Tallaght Resource Centre which has served many groups. Further help sought under Poverty 3 was not obtained, but the momentum of community development has been maintained by a special grant from the Irish government.

# Amsterdam Mid-North, Amsterdam, Netherlands

The area of Amsterdam to the north of the IJ river is known as Amsterdam North. For centuries it was used as a kind of 'overflow' for the city's problems or unwanted activities. At various times it was used as a gallows field, dump for canal and harbour sludge, site for heavy industry, housing for cheap labour and, in the 1970s, as an area for rehousing people from urban renewal areas in the city. In the 19th and much of the 20th century it was a vital part of Amsterdam's industrial economy, and it still is to some extent.

The bisecting of the area by the digging of the Noord Hollands Kanaal in 1824, and the establishment of engineering and chemical industries on the north bank of the IJ, set their seal on the development of 'Noord'. At first workers commuted to the industrial area but soon new housing estates were built. About a quarter of the houses in Noord were built between 1919 and 1930 and over a third between 1961 and 1970. Building is still going on, while older areas are being improved.

During the 1980s Amsterdam underwent a process of decentralisation of many of the city's powers and much of its budget to 16 largely autonomous districts. Since 1981 Amsterdam North, which occupies 28% of the geographical area of the city, has had its own council. The area is divided into three parts, of which mid-north is one. The population of Amsterdam North is almost 80,000, of which 32,000 are in Mid-North. The new council has sought to develop the area in a positive sense. Each locality contains a part of Old North and a part of New North, and has its own community development body.

In Amsterdam as a whole 29% of households have an income judged to be below the minimum necessary for reasonable living. Unemployment in Amsterdam is about 24%, with a heavy bias towards immigrant groups such as Surinamese, Antilleans, Turks and Moroccans. Poverty and disadvantage are concentrated in certain neighbourhoods.

Amsterdam North's economic dynamism, vital to the city for several generations, suffered some decline in the nineteen seventies and eighties. The shipping industry contracted and certain neighbourhoods were suddenly confronted with massive unemployment, though the average unemployment rate for North, at around 15%, is still lower than for Amsterdam as a whole. But the unemployment rate amongst ethnic minorities in North is 34%. The majority of unemployed tend to have poor educational qualifications, 50% of them are under 30, and 18% have been unemployed for over three years.

Amsterdam North has an undeservedly poor image which is difficult to shake off. The river Ij forms a psychological barrier. Although the Old North does have a low economic status, this is not true of the New North. The Old North is sometimes characterised as a typical working class area, the New North as a garden city, but these are oversimplifications.

The main features of the programme agreed by the district authorities for the next few years include social renewal, improving the environment and combatting unemployment, by developing 'socially desirable sectors' such as public transport, child minding, the caring occupations, social security and environmental management. The level of organisation of residents in Old North has traditionally been high, and residents have made a good deal of input to renewal plans, though many associations are now showing signs of 'ageing'. Social networks in New North are less evident, though residents come together over problems of subsidence and pollution. Other new initiatives include modernising the older industrial areas; a possible injection of help from the EC RENAVAL project; special efforts to keep the ship-repairing industry going; and ideas for a nautical trade exhibition and sports centre.

## Oliveira Do Douro, Oporto, Portugual

Oliveira do Douro is a 'freguesia' (civil parish) in the municipality of Vila Nova de Gaia, one of eight which comprise the recently-designated Metropolitan Area of Oporto (AMP), in northern Portugal. The freguesia is the smallest level of administration, with its own council, as set out in the new constitution following the political changes of 1974. The next largest is the municipality, and then the district. A number of districts make up a region. Regions were supposed to become increasingly autonomous, but continued centralisation and financial constraints have held this back.

Oliveira do Douro is situated on the left bank of the Douro, with the river forming its eastern boundary, and lies 6.5 km from the centre of Oporto. With 32,000 people, it is one of the most densely populated parts of the municipality.

For several decades industrialisation has served as a magnet for large numbers of workers from rural areas who have become concentrated in and around Portugal's main urban centres. Many people migrating to Oporto from northern and central Portugal settled here. The population of Oliveira do Douro has doubled in the past ten years, and the original rural nature of the parish has given way to a disorganised process of rapid urbanisation. Past economic activity consisted of fishing and small scale farming: water-mills and waterwheels stand as reminders. By 1952 the locality was home to more than 50 factories and workshops, many in the footwear industry but with some important engineering, transport and machinery plants. It continues to grow, and has become increasingly featureless.

Oliveira do Douro has an employment rate higher than average for the municipality, but 14% of households have no wage-earner and 29% have just one. Half the employed people are skilled or semi-skilled workers, and a further 30% are other workers in commerce, administration and the service sector. Officially the unemployment rate for the whole municipality is about 5% but there is probably a good deal of concealed unemployment and underemployment.

Housing and health conditions are not good. About half the population live in dwellings without a bathroom, and a quarter have no piped water. Litter is scattered around, and there are many open drains. The disordered growth of the housing stock has taken the form of many poorly designed high-rise blocks and a lack of adequate infrastructure. The great majority of the housing is rented, and little money is invested in maintenance. Cheap public housing for disadvantaged people has done little to alleviate the problems. Recently new private housing has begun to be constructed.

The area is so built up that there are few recreational spaces left, and the need for social centres and amenities has been bypassed. Meanwhile a new rail bridge has been constructed over the Douro. Some of its supports stand in the locality, and it will carry 400 trains a day. A road bridge is also planned, which is likely to cut across the residential locality. Existing roads date back to the time when the locality was a small rural one, and are very congested, whilst public transport, consisting of two privately-run bus services, is inadequate.

There are two health centres in Oliveira do Douro, one a state agency, the Centro de Saude, and one a private mutual-aid association. The Centro is the only source of free health care available to everyone. With twelve doctors and eight nurses, offering only primary health care, it is not able to meet everyone's needs. However, a new health Centre is nearing completion.

Oliveira do Douro has seven state primary schools, three of which are in poor condition, and two private ones. Secondary and technical education is located further afield but there are two community associations connected with secondary education. A variety of vocational training is available in the municipality, including some subsidised by the European Social Fund. Adult illiteracy is believed to be around 16%.

Plans for improvement include the construction of a sportsground and the setting up of a 'Local Technical Office' to co-ordinate the various municipal services in each civil parish, and tackle local problems. The parish council has high hopes that this will give people a greater say in local development and facilitate closer dialogue with the municipality.

# Can Serra, Barcelona, Spain

Can Serra is a neighbourhood situated in one of six districts which make up the town of Hospitalet del Llobregat, five kilometres south of Barcelona. It stands on an elevation in relation to the other parts of the town, which gives it a personality of its own.

After the fall of the dictatorship there was spectacular growth in the functions of the autonomous regional governments, especially regions like Catalonia with a historic national identity. The autonomous regional government (the Generalitat) has control over most sectors. In 1985 it abolished the Metropolitan Corporation of Barcelona (CMB) and set up area councils. Hospitalet is governed by a municipal council (Generalitat) some of whose responsibilities are devolved to the six district councils. One of these covers Can Serra and the adjoining neighbourhood of Pubilla Casas.

In the town plan of 1953, 50% of Can Serra was to be set aside as a town park, the rest to be a medium-density urban zone for migrants from elsewhere in Spain attracted by economic growth in the region. However speculative building was rife and by 1975 much of the neighbourhood had been built over, but with little of the necessary infrastructure of facilities to support the life of the new community.

The population of Hospitalet almost trebled between 1960 and 1981, from 123,000 to 295,000, making it Spain's tenth largest town and one of the most densely populated municipalities in the world. In the last decade there has been a slight reversal due largely to the end of the migration period and a stabilisation in the fertility rate. Growth in the Can Serra neighbourhood was even more dramatic, from less than 600 people before 1970, when the influx there began, to over 13,000 in 1990, about a twentieth of the population of Hospitalet. There are about 4000 households.

Can Serra is a dormitory neighbourhood with no industry of its own. Economic activity centres on the market, shops and services. Transport facilities are good. Commonest occupations are taxi-drivers, cleaning ladies and labourers. The older part of the neighbourhood consists mainly of small building plots, the newer part of high-rise blocks. With rents controlled by law until the mid 80's, most private building was for sale, not renting, and 90% of residents are in bought accommodation.

Forty-five per cent of Can Serra inhabitants are migrants from other regions of Spain, and 55% were born in Catalonia, most of these being the children of the migrants. Catalonia has its own language which has largely been assimilated by the new community. The average household now contains parents of early middle age and three children between five and twenty-five.

It is not typical for women to go out to work. 'Economic activity' rates are 54% amongst the male population and 18% amongst the female. Amongst these, there is 12% unemployment amongst the men, particularly young men, and 24% amongst the women. There is believed to be a fair amount of unregistered employment taking place, mainly of small repairs, domestic service and so on. Less than half the unemployed receive some kind of benefit, which in Spain depends on having worked for at least six months, receiving entitlement to benefits for three months for every six months worked, and a total limit of two years.

There are some major health problems in the neighbourhood. There is a marked incidence of alcohol and drug abuse, and there is a high percentage of disability.

# Thamesmead, London, UK

Thamesmead is a locality of approximately 28,500 people situated on the southern bank of the River Thames, twelve miles downstream from the centre of London. Although it is therefore near to some old areas of south London, it is almost entirely a 'new town', created in the 1960s on what was formerly marshland. Till the end of the second world war it was used for storing munitions from nearby Woolwich Arsenal, on artificially created small islands called 'tumps'. When these fell into disuse they became havens for wildlife, and a few have been preserved as environmental features. Draining some of the marshes provided what was then the largest area of building land available in the capital, with the added feature of several large lakes. Thamesmead is still surrounded to the east and west by marshland, and its approach road from the south is via an elevated highway. It therefore has a very separate character.

Begun in 1968, Thamesmead was originally managed by the Greater London Council (GLC) as an area of relatively cheap housing for rent, to ease accommodation pressures in other parts of the capital. With the abolition of the GLC in 1986 there was a dilemma as to what authority should become responsible for the settlement. Hitherto all the new towns created in Britain since the second world war, of which there had been 34, had passed into the governance of a local authority, existing or new. Thamesmead lies across the boundary of two such authorities, the London Boroughs of Greenwich and Bexley. (London is divided into 32 boroughs.) But the government was experimenting with new forms of privatisation, and a new kind of housing trust, Thamesmead Town, was created to manage the area as a private company. The two local authorities still have responsibility for other functions such as social services and education.

Thamesmead has continued to grow, and is still only half way towards its full planned population of 60,000. More houses are now built for sale than rent, and many tenants bought their houses at a discount under the government's 'right to buy' legislation in the 'eighties. Half the housing is now owner-occupied. Public transport is poor but there is little congestion. Car ownership is slightly lower than the national average.

Naturally most of the population have not lived in Thamesmead for very long. Compared with averages for the South East of England, one of Britain's most prosperous regions, people in Thamesmead are disadvantaged. Income is lower than average, unemployment, at 7%, slightly higher; more children have learning difficulties and the percentage of pupils staying in education after 16 is low. The physical and social conditions have many drawbacks. There has been little development of light industry, which had originally been planned. Everyday facilities such as shopping, entertainment and catering are poor, and the town is physically rather bleak.

Facilities differ somewhat as between the half of Thamesmead that is in Greenwich, a Labour authority, and that in Bexley, which is Conservative. For example day nursery places are available on the Greenwich side, but not on the Bexley side: local groups are pressing Bexley to create some. The incidence of health and mental health problems is high compared with Greenwich as a whole, and more so compared with Bexley as a whole.

Thamesmead has traditionally had fairly good educational provision, with thirteen primary schools, two secondary schools and a number of youth clubs and projects. But with the abolition of the Inner London Education Authority in 1988 (two years after that of the GLC), the youth centres and some general community projects have been faced with cutbacks of funding and face an uncertain future.

Thamesmead Town has put considerable effort into providing facilities for local groups and projects, which have grown fairly rapidly over the past ten years. But in 1990 and 91 several such initiatives were facing contraction or collapse, in common with many across the UK, due to funding crises and policy changes in public authorities.

# Chapter two
# People, localities and problems: the household survey

## Introduction

How do people in disadvantaged localities experience the problems of living there? What do they do about them? How does this relate to the role of public authorities and local groups? These were the main subject of the household survey carried out in the seven case-study localities.

The aim was to gain insight into:
- what people saw as the **main problem**s of the area
- where they **sought help** for problems affecting them
- whether they **took action** on local issues
- whether they knew about and were involved in **local groups**.

The main part of the survey was identical for all localities, as near as language would allow, and was carried out in a neighbourhood typical of the locality as a whole. Given the different local and national backgrounds, similarities are particularly interesting.

After national analysis, reported in the seven national studies, the figures were integrated into a single dataset, thereby enabling reanalysis and comparison. The tables in this chapter are from the combined reanalysis, against the background of information from the national studies, and a fuller report of the reanalysis is to be published separately.

The aim was to carry out 250 interviews in each locality, broadly balanced between men and women and different age-groups over 18. Actual numbers interviewed were:

| | |
|---|---|
| Sluizeken and Muide, Ghent, Belgium | 253 |
| Perama, Athens, Greece | 253 |
| Amsterdam Mid-North, Netherlands | 107 |
| Tallaght, Dublin, Ireland | 263 |
| Oliveira do Douro, Porto, Portugal | 251 |
| Can Serra, Barcelona, Spain | 250 |
| Thamesmead, London, United Kingdom | 218 |
| Total | 1,595 |

Where tables show the different localities, these numbers have been left as

*33*

they stand. Where tables show combined figures for the whole dataset, the numbers have been weighted to give equal representation to each locality on the basis of 250 units out of 1750; the figures in these tables therefore vary from the absolute numbers, in most cases only slightly but in the case of Amsterdam Mid-North considerably.

Each local survey had some specific national variations - either extra questions or occasionally a question omitted or asked in a different way. On some points, therefore, the data are not fully comparable. This is noted where it affects a particular table, and see also the technical note at the end of this chapter.

The localities are all urban areas in some way peripheral to an economic centre; are suffering certain disadvantages due to recent changes, such as rapid urbanisation or the decline of a traditional industry; and have also shown signs of community activity and adaptation to change. The material is therefore dealing with people having to cope with more than the average strain of contemporary urban life, in areas with distinct economic disadvantages and also in most cases rapid residential growth over the past 20 or more years. One effect of our choice of 'peripheral' localities to study was that rapid urbanisation at some point within recent decades turned out to be a major feature of social and economic change in most of these areas. The form this took was different from place to place: rapid expansion around an existing core, in Tallaght; expansion virtually obliterating the previous rural character, in Oliveira do Douro; building of new estates alongside renewal of old ones, in Amsterdam North; creation of a completely new town on formerly uninhabited land, in Thamesmead. Populations in most areas had therefore grown enormously over the past generation.

## The sample populations

A particular neighbourhood or part of each locality was selected for the household survey. The sample was structured to provide a balanced representation of adults from the age of 18 upwards, and of both sexes. The actual balance achieved varied slightly. The amount of detail collected on the characteristics of respondents in the sample areas was different from one national study to another and so it is difficult to give them in fully comparative form. The following selection provides an impression of the variety of local conditions:

In **Oliveira do Douro** (Portugal) 90% of respondents had been born in the region, 22% in the locality itself. 71% were married, and 60% had been living there for over 20 years. 64% had had four years' schooling or less. 5% had had higher education. 10% of households had one or more members looking for work.

As regards the type of household, it is interesting to note that 59% included relatives or friends as well as immediate family, whilst most of the rest were nuclear families alone. There were few single person households. There was considerable overcrowding. 11% were living in makeshift accommodation such as a shanty or converted garage. 27% did not have adequate bathroom facilities, and 25% had no telephone. 51% had a car.

In **Can Serra** (Spain) 33% of the respondents had been born in the province (Barcelona). These were mostly the under 35's. The over 35's had nearly all been born elsewhere, mainly Andalucia, Extremadura and Ciudad Real. Over half the respondents had been living there for 15-20 yrs.

89% of the homes were owner-occupied. There was no rented public housing sector. Most households had four (38%) or three (23%) people. Only 3% were single occupants. It is 'a neighbourhood largely inhabited by nuclear families, in which the heads of family were born in the poorest parts of Spain, received low levels of education, and had to emigrate to Barcelona where, between 1971 and 1975, they bought a flat in Can Serra. Most of them understand, but cannot speak, Catalan, but their children do. In general they have attained a middle class or lower middle class standard of comfort and usually have a telephone and a car' (S,45).

57% of respondents had completed less than six years' schooling. 6% had a medium or higher level qualification. 7.6% of the respondents were unemployed. 5% of households had no telephone. 80% had a car.

In **Amsterdam Mid-North** (Netherlands) the survey was carried out in Banne Buiksloot, a neighbourhood of 12,500 people. 14% of these were of non-Dutch origin, mainly Surinamese (Antilleans), Moroccans and Turks. Rather more women than men were interviewed. People of non-Dutch origin were under-represented.

50% of respondents had had no more than general primary or junior vocational education. A third of the sample had lived less than ten years in the neighbourhood. 82% of respondents were renting their homes.

In **Sluizeken/Muide** (Belgium) three quarters of the sample were of Belgian origin, and one quarter of Turkish origin. Just over half the respondents rented their homes, the remainder being owner-occupiers. A third of respondents had lived in the neighbourhood between six and ten years. 22% had lived there for more than 20 years. About 20% of respondents were unemployed.

Almost 70% of the Belgians interviewed lived alone or in a two person household, while only 8% of Turks did, with 57% living in households of more than five people.

In **Perama** (Greece) the survey was carried out in the eastern part of the locality. The majority of households in the neighbourhood were families consisting of married couples, for the most part with children living at home. 65% of respondents had had primary schooling only, or less. 6% had had further or higher education. 'The origin of a large number of the residents, especially the older ones, is from rural and semi-rural areas; Perama was formed mainly by the large waves of people migrating to the capital between 1945 and 1970. 21% of respondents were born in Perama' (G, 66). 10% of respondents were unemployed. One fifth of the sample households had no telephone. Two fifths had a car.

An area near the centre was selected for the survey in **Tallaght** (Ireland). Few of the respondents (3%) lived on their own. The great majority were in households with children. Just over half were living in public housing, whether rented or under a tenant purchase scheme, just under half in privately-owned homes. 46% of the sample had no formal educational qualifications, and 14% were unemployed.

The household survey in **Thamesmead** (UK) took place in its southern area. Two thirds of the sample were tenants of the housing authority, while one third owned their own homes. 18% of respondents lived on their own, 63% in households of two to four people and 19% in larger households. About four-fifths had had eleven years' education or more, 9% having had some form of higher education. Three-quarters of the sample had been born in

## Table 2.1
### Time of residence in locality

| Count Column % Time (Years) | Ghent Sl & M | Perama | Tallaght | Amster-dam N | Oliveira do Douro | Can Serra | Thames-mead | Total |
|---|---|---|---|---|---|---|---|---|
| <1 |  |  |  |  | 3 |  | 26 | 29 |
|  |  |  |  |  | 1.2 |  | 12.2 | 1.8 |
| 1–4 | 75 | 16 | 32 | 16 | 15 | 6 | 55 | 215 |
|  | 29.6 | 6.4 | 12.3 | 16.5 | 6 | 2.4 | 25.8 | 13.7 |
| 5–9 | 46 | 13 | 56 | 14 | 12 | 23 | 55 | 219 |
|  | 18.2 | 5.2 | 21.5 | 14.4 | 4.8 | 9.2 | 25.8 | 13.9 |
| 10–19 | 64 | 50 | 141 | 54 | 74 | 131 | 60 | 574 |
|  | 25.3 | 20 | 54.2 | 55.7 | 29.5 | 52.4 | 28.2 | 36.5 |
| 20–29 | 30 | 67 | 28 | 10 | 60 | 65 | 14 | 274 |
|  | 11.9 | 26.8 | 10.8 | 10.3 | 23.9 | 26 | 6.6 | 17.4 |
| 30+ | 38 | 104 | 3 | 3 | 87 | 25 | 3 | 263 |
|  | 15 | 41.6 | 1.2 | 3.1 | 34.7 | 10 | 1.4 | 16.7 |
| Column Total | 253 | 250 | 260 | 97 | 251 | 250 | 213 | 1574 |
|  | 16.1 | 15.9 | 16.5 | 6.2 | 15.9 | 15.9 | 13.5 | 100 |

the UK, others being from Ireland, elsewhere in Europe, Africa and Vietnam. 12% of respondents were unemployed - higher than the average for the locality and the region. Access to a car, at 56%, and a telephone, at 79%, were low compared to UK averages.

Length of residence of the samples can be compared for all the localities: almost two thirds of the household survey sample in Thamesmead had lived there for less than ten years, half the sample in Ghent and a third in Tallaght and Amsterdam Mid-North. Only in Perama and Oliveira do Douro had more than half the sample populations lived there for over twenty years (**Table 2.1**).

## Problems and issues

People in the seven localities saw themselves as facing a range of problems. These were explored in different ways: first open-endedly, then prompted

### Table 2.2
### Unprompted issues by locality

| Count % Repondents | Ghent SI & M | Perama | Tallaght | Amsterdam N | Oliveira do Douro | Can Serra | Thamesmead | Row Total |
|---|---|---|---|---|---|---|---|---|
| Transport | 33 | 96 | 40 | 6 | 118 | 69 | 9 | 371 |
|  | 27.3 | 23.3 | 5.3 | 2.8 | 26.2 | 17 | 4.5 | 14.5 |
| Housing | 2 | 1 | 3 | 26 | 32 | 28 | 13 | 105 |
|  | 1.7 | 0.2 | 0.4 | 12.1 | 7.1 | 6.9 | 6.5 | 4.1 |
| Education | 5 | 37 | 19 |  | 10 | 20 | 11 | 102 |
|  | 4.1 | 9 | 2.5 |  | 2.2 | 4.9 | 5.5 | 4 |
| Environment | 49 | 202 | 284 | 147 | 178 | 124 | 105 | 1089 |
|  | 40.5 | 49 | 37.8 | 68.4 | 39.5 | 30.6 | 52.2 | 42.6 |
| Health |  | 12 | 30 |  | 1 | 91 | 3 | 137 |
|  |  | 2.9 | 4 |  | 0.2 | 22.5 | 1.5 | 5.4 |
| Employment |  | 7 | 202 |  | 6 | 1 | 4 | 220 |
|  |  | 1.7 | 26.9 |  | 1.3 | 0.2 | 2 | 8.6 |
| Other | 32 | 57 | 173 | 36 | 106 | 72 | 56 | 532 |
|  | 26.4 | 13.8 | 23 | 16.7 | 23.5 | 17.8 | 27.9 | 20.8 |
| Column Total | 121 | 412 | 751 | 215 | 451 | 405 | 201 | 2556 |
|  | 4.7 | 16.1 | 29.4 | 8.4 | 17.6 | 15.8 | 7.9 | 100 |

Note: Cell contents represent count of issues raised and the percent of total issues, not respondents.

**Table 2.3**
**Prompted issues by locality**

| Count % Respondents Issue | Ghent Sl & M | Perama | Oliveira do Douro | Can Serra | Thamesmead | Row Total |
|---|---|---|---|---|---|---|
| Transport | 131 | 146 | 114 | 21 | 92 | 504 |
|  | 25.2 | 24.6 | 25.8 | 4.2 | 32.9 | 21.6 |
| Housing | 124 | 12 | 117 | 85 | 31 | 369 |
|  | 24.0 | 2.0 | 27.6 | 17.1 | 11.1 | 15.8 |
| Education | 47 | 75 | 30 | 57 | 28 | 237 |
|  | 9.0 | 12.6 | 7.0 | 11.4 | 10.0 | 11.0 |
| Environment | 131 | 201 | 38 | 117 | 64 | 551 |
|  | 25.2 | 33.8 | 9.0 | 23.5 | 22.9 | 23.6 |
| Health | 27 | 111 | 55 | 99 | 26 | 318 |
|  | 5.2 | 18.9 | 13.0 | 20.0 | 9.9 | 13.6 |
| Employment | 60 | 49 | 70 | 119 | 39 | 337 |
|  | 11.5 | 8.2 | 16.5 | 23.9 | 13.9 | 14.4 |
| Totals | 520 | 594 | 424 | 498 | 280 | 2337 |
|  | 23.1 | 25.4 | 18.1 | 21.3 | 12.0 | 100 |

Note: Cell contents represent count of issues agreed with and percent of respondents. Tallaght and Amsterdam not included here since question was not asked in this form.

by a list of issues already identified as being some of the key issues in European social policy. To avoid duplication when recording the prompted replies, information was only counted if the respondent had not already mentioned the problem previously. Answers were grouped under the prepared headings (**Tables 2.2 and 2.3**). Most people throughout saw themselves or someone in their household as directly affected by the problems they had identified.

**Environment** (including the physical condition of the neighbourhood) emerged as the commonest problem overall, both unprompted and prompted. It was also highest for most localities individually. For several the next most prominent problem was **transport**. In Thamesmead not many people nominated transport as a problem until prompted, but then emphatically did so. In Perama, few nominated housing, despite huge housing problems. The Greek report suggests this is because housing in Greece is not seen as a public responsibility, and therefore in this kind of investigation people would not identify it as a public issue.

The truest picture of which problem areas most concerned people is

Environment was the problem most frequently cited by people in the case-study localities. Abandoned cars like these in Tallaght (Ireland, top) and Can Serra (Spain, left) are a recurrent motif in many peripheral areas.

## Table 2.4
### Combined issues by locality

| Count % Issues / Issue | Ghent SI & M | Perama | Oliveira do Douro | Can Serra | Thames-mead | Row Total |
|---|---|---|---|---|---|---|
| Transport | 164 | 242 | 232 | 90 | 101 | 829 |
|  | 25.6 | 25.5 | 30.0 | 10.8 | 23.7 | 22.9 |
| Housing | 126 | 13 | 149 | 113 | 44 | 445 |
|  | 19.7 | 1.4 | 19.4 | 13.6 | 10.4 | 12.3 |
| Education | 52 | 112 | 40 | 77 | 39 | 320 |
|  | 8.9 | 11.8 | 5.2 | 9.3 | 9.2 | 8.9 |
| Environment | 180 | 403 | 216 | 241 | 169 | 1209 |
|  | 28.1 | 42.5 | 28.1 | 29.0 | 39.8 | 33.4 |
| Health | 27 | 123 | 56 | 190 | 29 | 425 |
|  | 4.2 | 12.7 | 7.3 | 22.9 | 6.8 | 11.8 |
| Employment | 92 | 56 | 76 | 120 | 43 | 387 |
|  | 14.4 | 5.9 | 9.9 | 24.4 | 10.1 | 10.7 |
| Totals | 641 | 949 | 769 | 831 | 425 | 3615 |
|  | 17.7 | 26.3 | 21.3 | 23.0 | 11.8 | 100 |

Note: Cell contents represent count of issues agreed with and percent of respondents. Tallaght and Amsterdam not included here since question was not asked in this form.

probably obtained by considering both the prompted and unprompted responses. This gives the picture in **Table 2.4**. The combined responses (which are limited to comparative information on five localities) show the problems which people nominated spontaneously plus those which they endorsed when mentioned to them. These frequently reinforced the prominence of environmental issues, whilst some other issues jumped in importance, as if they had not been at the front of people's minds but once mentioned were readily recognised.

Greater detail on how people valued their locality and how they saw its problems can be gleaned from the descriptions in the national studies. In **Oliveira do Douro** (Portugal), 59% broadly liked the locality, and the figure was higher for those who had lived there longest. What they liked was 'the peace, the village atmosphere' or 'relationships with other people'. Those who disliked it were less specific. Environment was a key problem, including sanitation, pollution, roads and lack of green spaces.

The second most prominent problem was housing and the third transport:

poor bus services, safety, the state of repair of buses, and the cost. 'These problems were often attributed to the 'monopoly' of public transport held by private enterprises without, according to several respondents and the relevant policy-maker, checks or regulations' (P 54).

Most respondents in **Can Serra** (Spain) liked it, for being a quiet, pleasant neighbourhood, and for the local people. A high value was placed on the range of shops, the fact that things were close at hand. 7% liked nothing at all about it, and many of these were among the more elderly.

Environment was again the main problem, followed by jobs. Dirt and noise (22%), parking and traffic (20%), drugs and insecurity (16%) reinforced this concern. 10% of respondents were concerned about conflicts between neighbours.

The proportion of respondents who liked **Perama** (Greece) was a little over 50%. What they mainly liked was the view, the atmosphere and being outside the congested central areas of the city. 90% of respondents identified problems, mostly more than one. 49% of problems were to do with environment: pollution, poor infrastructure and lack of town planning. 23% of problems were to do with transport and communications, the difficulty of access to Athens and so to jobs and facilities. 14% of problems had to do with lack of shops and services, and with risks arising from shipbuilding and repair yards, with their fuel and gas storage. Further problems were to do with education.

In **Thamesmead** (UK) 78% of respondents liked something about the locality. These included 'quality of life' factors like the surroundings, greenery, quietness and lack of pollution; good neighbours and 'good community spirit'. However, 75% thought people outside the area had a bad image of it.

Three fifths of respondents mentioned problems spontaneously, mostly more than one. Nearly half the unprompted problems were about antisocial behaviour by other people: crime, vandalism, drugs and delinquency. Next largest, at 16%, were environmental issues like uncontrolled dogs, pollution, litter, smells and noise. A gender and age difference emerged from these concerns: 'Women were more concerned about antisocial behaviour and racism than men, and were also more concerned about facilities for children. Older people tended to be more worried by antisocial behaviour whilst the younger age group were more concerned by racism' (U,5.3).

42% of the sample felt that facilities were inadequate. 28% wanted better amenities such as shopping and services, 24% better provision for children and young people and child care support.

When problems were prompted, the Poll Tax was by far the largest issue, endorsed by 62% of the sample. Next largest was transport: women, and households with no car, were more likely to identify transport than men.

An additional 29% of the sample endorsed environment. Housing, education, health and employment were endorsed by between 14% and 18% each.

95% of respondents mentioned problems in **Amsterdam Mid-North** (Holland). Dirt and pollution were the most prominent, then crime and vandalism, unpleasant smells, poor housing maintenance, and traffic congestion:

Regarding the environment, there was a major problem with litter: 'The problem is litter on the streets, squares, shopping centre, parks and other open places. Fifteen of the respondents were actively working on it - going to meetings and campaigning, or rolling up their own sleeves, individually or with a group. Residents' committees from the housing associations, tenants' committees, special interest groups of landlords and the Banne South Working Groups were all working on this problem, according to the respondents' (N,111).

With crime and vandalism the problems were larceny, picking pockets, burglary, hooliganism, destruction of property and graffiti. As regards traffic, 'the problems were wrongly parked cars, the dangers and noise produced by fast cars and motor cycles tearing around.... The vast majority thought nothing could be done about it. A few had reported it to some official body. In addition to the district council, volunteers at the community centre were also trying to improve the situation' (N,112).

A majority of respondents in **Sluizeken/Mulde** (Belgium) attributed positive characteristics to their district. 'On closer perusal, there were considerable differences between population categories: young people and the self-employed were on average more negative about the district. Elderly people and people of Turkish origin were more positive. In particular, single people, women and the elderly felt the district to be dangerous' (B,3.4).

Traffic and the living environment were experienced as a problem by just over half the respondents, and housing by just under half. Conflict between Belgians and migrants concerned somewhat fewer, followed by employment, social life, education, training and health.

In **Tallaght** (Ireland) a proportion of respondents liked the facilities, the environment, the education, the location, and good neighbours, but 20% felt negative about the area, and 37% did not feel involved in what went on in their neighbourhood. 52% spontaneously nominated three or more problems. Lack of services, unemployment and crime were all mentioned by about a quarter of respondents, followed by roads and transport, poor public image of Tallaght, housing and environment, education and health.

# Methods of coping: responses to problems

What were people doing about the problems they had identified? In many cases they had done nothing within the past year, in others they had discussed it with people, collected information, gone to a meeting, been active in a group, raised it with the authorities or taken some other action. These responses were grouped into those which were not significantly active outside the household (nothing, discussed or collected information) and those which were (going to a meeting, group or institution). Overall, about **a quarter of the sample had done something active in the community about a problem during the past year**. The variations are shown in **Table 2.5**. In Perama, almost half the sample had been active in the community

## Table 2.5
### Active on one or more issues by locality

| Count Column % Active? | Ghent Sl & M | Perama | Tallaght | Amster-dam N | Oliveira do Douro | Can Serra | Thames-mead | Row Total |
|---|---|---|---|---|---|---|---|---|
| Not Active | 197 | 135 | 199 | 100 | 211 | 203 | 162 | 1207 |
|  | 77.9 | 54.0 | 76.0 | 93.5 | 84.1 | 81.2 | 74.3 | 75.6 |
| Active | 56 | 115 | 63 | 7 | 40 | 47 | 56 | 384 |
|  | 22.1 | 46.0 | 24.0 | 6.5 | 15.9 | 18.8 | 25.7 | 24.1 |
| Column | 253 | 250 | 262 | 107 | 251 | 250 | 218 | 1591 |

on at least one problem. The figures for Tallaght and Thamesmead were similar at about a quarter, with Can Serra and Oliveira do Douro at about a fifth and a sixth respectively.

What influenced people to be either more or less active on issues? It is hard to come to any conclusions about people who did not nominate problems. This could have been for widely differing reasons: on the one hand that they were content with things as they were; on the other, that they were too immersed in problems to see them clearly as problems **of the locality**. Community work experience shows that for many people in disadvantaged situations the disadvantages are experienced personally, conflated with the individual's self-concept and difficulties in surviving, and are not seen as objective or collective problems in the locality. The idea that such problems can be shared and acted on, and that they are in fact the object of public policy, comes as a revelation - sometimes a liberating one - to many of the people most affected. It is therefore very likely that many of those who did not nominate problems nor were active on them were nevertheless affected by them.

What can be seen is how far people who did see problems as being of public concern were active on them in the community. This is of critical interest to us, since one of the main objects of policies which seek to 'involve the local inhabitant' is to maximise this willingness on the part of residents to

### Table 2.6
### Active on one or more issues by sex and locality

| Count Sex Nos. Active | Ghent SI & M | Perama | Tallaght | Amster-dam N | Oliveira do Douro | Can Serra | Thames-mead | Row Total |
|---|---|---|---|---|---|---|---|---|
| Male | 42 | 65 | 37 | 2 | 27 | 23 | 25 | 221 |
|  | 22.5 | 52.0 | 28.2 | 5.0 | 21.6 | 18.1 | 24.8 | 26.4 |
| Female | 13 | 50 | 26 | 5 | 13 | 24 | 31 | 162 |
|  | 20.0 | 40.0 | 19.8 | 7.9 | 10.3 | 19.5 | 26.5 | 21.6 |
| Total | 55 | 115 | 63 | 7 | 40 | 47 | 56 | 383 |
| % Total | 21.8 | 46.0 | 24.0 | 6.8 | 15.9 | 18.8 | 25.7 | 24.1 |

Note: Cell contents are counts of each sex active on one or more issues, and percent of that sex active. Percent of total figure is proportion of all respondents active on one or more issues.

### Table 2.7
### Active on one or more issues by age and locality

| Count % Age Nos. active | Ghent SI & M | Perama | Tallaght | Amster-dam N | Oliveira do Douro | Thames-mead | Total % Total |
|---|---|---|---|---|---|---|---|
| Up To 39 | 19 | 56 | 26 | 2 | 16 | 34 | 153 |
|  | 19.2 | 47.5 | 17.9 | 5.4 | 15.8 | 24.8 | 24.0 |
| 40 to 59 | 25 | 42 | 32 | 4 | 15 | 14 | 132 |
|  | 28.7 | 51.9 | 33.3 | 8.9 | 19.7 | 30.4 | 30.6 |
| 60 plus | 11 | 17 | 5 | 1 | 9 | 8 | 51 |
|  | 17.5 | 33.3 | 23.8 | 4.0 | 12.2 | 22.9 | 19.0 |
| Total | 55 | 115 | 63 | 7 | 40 | 56 | 336 |
| % Total | 22.1 | 46.0 | 24.0 | 6.5 | 15.9 | 25.7 | 25.1 |

Note: Can Serra not included here due to unavailabilty of age data. Cell contents are counts of each age group active on one or more issues, and percent of that group active. Percent of total figure is proportion of all respondents active on one or more issues.

## Table 2.8
## Active on one or more issues by time in locality, and locality

| Count % Time Nos. Active Years | Ghent Sl & M | Perama | Tallaght | Amster-dam N | Oliveira do Douro | Can Serra | Thames-mead | Row Total |
|---|---|---|---|---|---|---|---|---|
| 0-4 | 13 | 6 | 4 |  | 2 | 2 | 14 | 41 |
|  | 17.3 | 37.5 | 12.5 |  | 11.1 | 33.3 | 17.3 | 16.8 |
| 5-9 | 11 | 9 | 9 |  | 2 | 4 | 19 | 54 |
|  | 23.9 | 69.2 | 16.1 |  | 16.7 | 17.4 | 34.5 | 24.7 |
| 10-19 | 16 | 30 | 38 | 4 | 9 | 32 | 17 | 146 |
|  | 25.0 | 60.0 | 27.0 | 7.4 | 12.2 | 24.4 | 28.3 | 25.4 |
| 20-29 | 9 | 28 | 11 | 1 | 11 | 5 | 5 | 70 |
|  | 30.0 | 41.8 | 39.3 | 10.0 | 18.3 | 7.7 | 35.7 | 25.5 |
| 30+ | 7 | 42 | 1 | 1 | 16 | 4 |  | 71 |
|  | 18.4 | 40.4 | 33.3 | 33.3 | 18.4 | 16.0 |  | 27.0 |
| Total | 56 | 115 | 63 | 6 | 40 | 47 | 55 | 382 |
| % Total | 22.1 | 46.0 | 24.2 | 6.2 | 15.9 | 18.8 | 25.8 | 24.3 |

Note: Cell contents are counts of each group active on one or more issues, and percent of that group active. Percent of total figure is proportion of all respondents active on one or more issues.

be active on problems in the locality. What are the factors that influence whether people are more or less active? Are they age; gender; length of residence in the locality? (**Tables 2.6, 2.7 and 2.8**).

Rather more men than women were active on issues outside the household overall (about a quarter to a fifth), with variations between similar proportions in Thamesmead, Can Serra and Sluizeken/Muide and a more marked preponderance of men in Tallaght, Perama and most of all in Oliveira do Douro. This is perhaps surprising, since much of the information in this study shows women to have a more significant role in many ways. On the other hand, this is often a somewhat hidden role, and balanced by the higher profile often taken by men when they get involved. The role of women was often far greater in private household activity and in the lower-profile aspects of public action, whilst men tended to take the higher profile roles such as the officer positions in local organisations. In Oliveira do Douro the role of women in local activity was often described as almost a concealed one; in Tallaght, analysis showed that the few paid posts in local organisations more often tended to go to men even in organisations whose members were predominantly women. But since, overall, involvement in groups and organisations is remarkably balanced between the sexes (see

*45*

Table 2.11 below) much of the difference must come from a higher degree of men's action outside groups.

The age pattern echoes information received from groups. **The most active age is between about 30 and 50**. This is consistent in all the localities. In five of the six cases the next most active are the younger group, the exception being Tallaght, but the numbers of elderly there are too small to draw conclusions. Nevertheless, an appreciable proportion of the elderly are still active - around a fifth in Sluizekjen/Muide, Tallaght and Thamesmead, an eighth in Oliveira and fully a third in Perama.

The age factor almost certainly relates to other things known about how local action works. To participate in local action, especially in a disadvantaged area, you need to see yourself as committed to that area, committed to improving conditions over a period of time, not only for yourself and your family as individuals but for local society in general. Young people are less likely to be able to take this long view, and often see themselves, realistically or not, as seeking to escape from disadvantage by moving elsewhere. A great deal of local action evidently arises from the caring role of women, which develops perhaps most when they have children and those children are getting to school age. Old people, on the other hand, are less likely to be willing or able to go out to meetings in the evenings and in general are likely to be less mobile.

Length of residence in the locality had some bearing on whether people were active on local affairs. Whilst an appreciable number were active within their first five years, the proportion then increased, and then remained fairly constant. In Sluizeken/Muide and Tallaght, activity seemed to increase fairly steadily with length of residence, dropping off again a little after 30 years. In other localities it fluctuated somewhat more with length of residence. It appears therefore that some people become active soon after their arrival in an area but that longer residence encourages activity for rather more people.

## Involvement in groups

How did people's attitudes to local problems and readiness to be active on them relate to the life of local groups? First, people were asked generally about their involvement in, or use of, the whole range of different types of group - not just the 'social issue' groups which were of particular concern in relation to social policy. In order to get a picture of how many people were involved in any groups at all, helpers and users of any group were combined ('involved') and distinguished from those who neither helped nor used any group or did so only marginally ('not involved much'). **Almost half the sample population overall were involved in at least one group (Table 2.9)**. Involvement was high in Thamesmead, well over 50% in Tallaght, Can Serra and Amsterdam Mid-North, and around a third in Sluizeken/Muide, Perama and Oliveira do Douro.

### Table 2.9
### Involvement with one or more local groups by locality

| Count Column % | Ghent SI & M | Perama | Tallaght | Amsterdam N | Oliveira do Douro | Can Serra | Thamesmead | Row Total |
|---|---|---|---|---|---|---|---|---|
| **Involved** | 105 | 87 | 159 | 55 | 75 | 140 | 173 | **739** |
|  | 41.5 | 34.8 | 60.7 | 51.4 | 29.9 | 56.0 | 79.4 | **46.4** |
| **Not involved** | 148 | 163 | 103 | 52 | 176 | 110 | 45 | **852** |
|  | 58.5 | 65.2 | 39.3 | 48.6 | 70.1 | 44.0 | 20.6 | **53.6** |
| **Column** | **253** | **250** | **262** | **107** | **251** | **250** | **218** | **1591** |

### Table 2.10
### Variability of involvement in groups

| Count Column % Involved? | Sports, leisure & arts | Religious | Political | Community | Tenant/resident | Social clubs | Trade unions & others | average % |
|---|---|---|---|---|---|---|---|---|
| **Not involved** | 1035 | 1108 | 1219 | 1160 | 1196 | 924 | 1025 |  |
|  | 75.8 | 81.7 | 89.6 | 85.9 | 88.9 | 85.2 | 83.7 | **84.6** |
| **Don't do much** | 51 | 62 | 77 | 76 | 66 | 41 | 101 |  |
|  | 3.7 | 4.6 | 5.7 | 5.6 | 4.1 | 3.8 | 8.3 | **5.2** |
| **Use them** | 166 | 130 | 18 | 40 | 47 | 93 | 65 |  |
|  | 12.2 | 9.6 | 1.3 | 3.0 | 3.5 | 8.6 | 5.3 | **6.2** |
| **Help organise** | 57 | 28 | 32 | 47 | 20 | 16 | 17 |  |
|  | 4.2 | 2.1 | 2.4 | 3.5 | 1.3 | 1.5 | 1.4 | **2.4** |
| **Use and help** | 53 | 26 | 11 | 25 | 13 | 7 | 13 |  |
|  | 3.9 | 1.9 | 0.8 | 1.6 | 0.8 | 0.6 | 0.8 | **1.6** |
| **Total** | **1362** | **1354** | **1357** | **1348** | **1342** | **1081** | **1221** |  |

**Table 2.10** shows the pattern of involvement in greater detail. Much of the involvement was in sports, social, cultural and religious groups as well as in community, tenants' and residents' groups. No one type of group involved more than a quarter of the sample; most attracted between 10 and 20% involvement. A rough idea of the degree of overlap can be obtained from the fact that 46% of the sample altogether are actively involved in one or more groups (Table 2.9). Evidently, then, many are involved in several groups, whilst just over half the sample is not involved in any.

Evidently a wide variety of types of group is necessary to ensure that people have sufficient opportunity to get involved. It should be stressed that not all these types of groups were equally available in all localities: non-involvement may reflect non-availability rather than lack of interest. The non-participation of 54% of the sample suggests that the range of groups in many of the localities was too small, probably both as to subject-matter and accessibility, to reach all those who could have benefitted.

The figures in Table 2.10 can also be used to get an impression of the relation of helping to using. A group which has much overlap between helpers and users could be regarded as highly participative. A group where helpers and users are more separate could be regarded as more of a service to others. The following ratios of helping to using have been obtained by adding the numbers who use a group to those who both use and help, and comparing this figure with another figure obtained by adding the numbers who help a group to those who both use and help. Thus those who both use and help are here counted twice, to reflect their double involvement.

| Sport/<br>Arts/<br>Leisure | Religious | Political | Community | Residents | Social | Trades<br>union<br>and other |
|---|---|---|---|---|---|---|
| 1:2 | 1:3 | 3:2 | 1:1 | 1:2 | 1:4 | 1:3 |

These proportions suggest that **most groups are to some extent 'self-help' groups**, providing considerable opportunities for participation as well as benefitting from a service. It is notable that over a third of the people involved in sports, leisure and arts groups are active in organising or helping them, similar to the proportion in tenants' and residents' groups, which attract far less involvement. Religious groups attract considerable usage, with an appreciable proportion of active members, whilst the proportion of active members in social clubs is rather lower. An important implication for policy is that to **achieve widespread participation it is necessary to have many types of group available**, including sports, leisure, arts and religious groups as well as those dealing specifically with local issues.

Table 2.10 can also be seen as suggesting a pattern of 'concentric circles' of involvement, which recurs later in analysis of groups themselves. At the core of group activity are between 2% and 8% of people who are involved in organising or running the group, and half or more of these also benefit from the use of the group. Another circle, usually rather larger, are other people who use the services of the group - mostly between 3% and 12%. A further circle see themselves as 'involved but not much' - occasional users or helpers. For each specific type of group, this leaves a majority uninvolved at all, though it will be seen from some of the group achievements described in the next chapter that people benefit from groups in ways that they are unaware of, such as the establishment of amenities and the monitoring of public services.

In general, sport, leisure, arts, religious and social groups were the most used, and branches of political parties least. This may simply reflect the fact that people do not see local political party groups as providing direct services or involvement in the locality, and indeed comments from some users, particularly in Perama, Can Serra and Oliveira do Douro, suggested that people thought that local action groups should not be tied up with party politics. This was a quite separate issue from whether groups took 'political' action 'with a small "p"', i.e. campaigning, mobilising or lobbying for a particular objective.

Taking a closer look at how involvement is affected by various factors, it is

### Table 2.11
### Involvement in one or more local groups by sex

| Count Column % Involved? | Male | Female | Row Total |
|---|---|---|---|
| Involved 1+ | 444 | 414 | 858 |
|  | 49.6 | 49.1 | 49.3 |
| Not involved | 541 | 430 | 882 |
|  | 50.4 | 50.9 | 50.7 |
| Column Total | 896 | 844 | 1740 |
|  | 51.2 | 48.3 | 100.0 |

### Table 2.12
### Involvement in one or more local groups by age

| Count Column % Involved? | Up To 39 | 40 to 59 | 60 plus | Row total |
|---|---|---|---|---|
| Involved 1+ | 363 | 243 | 118 | 725 |
|  | 52.0 | 49.4 | 38.8 | 48.5 |
| Not involved | 335 | 249 | 187 | 771 |
|  | 48.0 | 50.6 | 61.2 | 51.5 |
| Column Total | 698 | 492 | 306 | 1496 |
|  | 46.7 | 32.9 | 20.4 | 100.0 |

## Table 2.13
### Involvement in one or more local groups by time in locality

| Count Column % Involved? | <1 | 1-4 | 5-9 | 10-19 | 20-29 | 30+ | Row Total |
|---|---|---|---|---|---|---|---|
| Involved 1+ | 27 | 111 | 142 | 349 | 128 | 88 | 845 |
|  | 83.4 | 46.0 | 58.6 | 53.9 | 44.5 | 32.9 | 49.2 |
| Not involved | 5 | 131 | 101 | 299 | 160 | 179 | 874 |
|  | 16.6 | 54.0 | 41.4 | 46.1 | 55.5 | 67.1 | 50.8 |
| Column Total | 33 | 242 | 243 | 647 | 288 | 267 | 1719 |
|  | 1.9 | 14.1 | 14.1 | 37.7 | 16.7 | 15.5 | 100.0 |

(Time in Locality (years))

found that male and female involvement is on average virtually equal (**Table 2.11**). Involvement is also fairly constant at different ages, falling off a little after the age of 60, but even then remaining fairly substantial (**Table 2.12**). It is interesting to compare this with length of time in the locality (**Table 2.13**). What seems to happen is that a great majority of new arrivals try out some involvement within their first year, after which nearly half drop out. Between one and ten years of residence involvement creeps up again, and then more or less stabilises till it begins to fall off again after around 20 to 30 years' residence, no doubt affected in some cases by age and mobility.

A more detailed impression of some of the factors underlying involvement and non-involvement can be gained from the national studies. The following examples throw some light, for example, on areas where women or men are more involved, on how people heard about groups and about what motivated them or stopped them from getting involved.

In **Can Serra**, for the central age group women participate more in parents' and residents' associations, men in political parties and trade unions. For younger people (under 35) the gender spread was fairly equal. This was one of several indicators in that locality of a changing trend away from gender-specific roles.

In **Sluizeken/Mulde**, men were more often (45%) than women (30%) members of one or more societies or groups. The most popular were sports, religious, social and cultural groups. The six best known local organisations were known to between a third and two thirds of the sample. More were known in their immediate locality and to their specific target groups. Most respondents had first heard of the the local groups/organisations through friends, neighbours and acquaintances. Others were known because respondents had seen them, and to a lesser extent through publicity and printed information.

Being active in a local group was a prime form of action in **Tallaght**: 'Involvement in a local group or initiative was the most frequently reported form of action among those who reported doing something about issues they had identified' (I,63). Those who were employed were more likely to take action than those unemployed or not in the labour force. However, it was also in households with children and particularly lone parent households that one found a higher proportion of residents reporting that they had taken action (47% compared with 29% of other categories).

A higher proportion of men were involved in sports clubs and of women in community and adult education groups. People were more active if they were personally affected by an issue, if they saw the neighbourhood as more than just a place to live in, if they had friends among their neighbours, if they were more aware of local groups, and if they had lived there longer. Regarding how they had heard of groups, in 21% of cases it had been from friends or neighbours, 25% from notices, 22% from local media, 13% from seeing the premises.

The attitudes of some of those who got actively involved in groups are illustrated in these quotations from local people: "'If you see something that needs to be done in your community, problems or something that's wrong, really what can you do but do something about it. It's your community, you've got to deal with it. And anyway, if you make things better for your community, they're better for your family as well.'" (I,76). "'I had been using the group for a while and really got a lot out of it. When I found out that they needed people to become involved, I realised that if I didn't get involved, then it would just cease to exist, and I didn't want that'" (I,77).

The Tallaght study also went further to examine reasons given by respondents for *non*-involvement. These revealed a strong gender pattern, with commitments to the home and family featuring large for women, but in all cases lack of interest or awareness of groups being less important than other impediments. This suggests that people might be a lot more involved if conditions were more favourable.

| % | women | men | |
|---|---|---|---|
| family/domestic | 38 | 16 | |
| employment | 17 | 28 | |
| other commitments | 11 | 17 | |
| not interested | 19 | 19 | |
| not aware of groups | 2 | 9 | |
| ill health/old age | 4 | 6 | |
| N | 82 | 93 | (I,77) |

In **Thamesmead** there was a particularly wide contrast between the high use of groups for social, recreational, sporting and religious purposes and their use as a recourse for solving problems. 'These results seem to show that without better knowledge of their existence and activities, groups and organsations remain a limited option for most people, despite unsatisfactory alternatives. This is not surprising in the light of the small size of many of the (social issue) groups, and lack of knowledge of them... There was evidently little understanding of the potential of groups for influencing authorities as well as for direct provision of some kind of help or activity' (U,5.13)

An interesting feature in Thamesmead was that, unusually in this study, it had an umbrella group which aimed to give help to *all* the groups in the locality and had had a major influence in the development of the local groups sector but was known to few people: 'In terms of its importance in Thamesmead it was striking that only 14 respondents had heard of Trust Thamesmead. Presumably this relates to the fact that its members are the other local groups rather than individuals; but it still seems to be a dangerously low profile for what is in many ways the key group in the whole area, on which many of the others depend and which created many of the local facilities' (U,5.13).

There was a striking lack of connection between the fact that many people wanted better facilities in the area and the historical fact that many of the facilities that did exist had been achieved through Trust Thamesmead and some of the groups it had helped to set up. 'The process by which groups could influence and interact with authorities was evidently understood only by a small circle of those involved, and once facilities did exist they were probably seen as having been provided for, and belonging to, the local authorities rather than local people and their organisations' (U,5.13).

## General groups and social issue groups

It has been said earlier that the choice of groups to survey and focus on had been influenced by the assumption that groups tackling a specific social issue were more relevant to social policy than groups merely existing to provide a recreational, sporting or religious facility. The above figures on involvement, combined with closer knowledge of groups, which emerges in subsequent chapters, suggest that this differentiation should not be made too rigidly. Evidently a good deal of informal problem-solving, social cohesion and information-exchange took place in any kind of group, even if it was not an explicit part of that group's aims; and it appears also that the satisfaction of helping to organise activity was found by many people in recreational, sporting or religious rather than 'social issue' groups. Further, the analysis of groups shows that in some localities, mutual support and the resolution of problems was sometimes just as, or more, likely to be taking place under a recreational heading as under a 'community' one.

It remains true, though, that whilst all kinds of group are important for

## Table 2.14
## Number of eight named groups known

| Count Column % No. Known | Ghent Sl & M | Perama | Tallaght | Amsterdam N | Oliveira do Douro | Can Serra | Thamesmead | Row Total |
|---|---|---|---|---|---|---|---|---|
| Know none | 59 | 7 | 4 | 24 | 1 | 17 | 28 | 140 |
|  | 23.3 | 2.8 | 1.5 | 22.4 | 0.4 | 6.8 | 12.8 | 8.8 |
| Know 1 | 64 | 22 | 2 | 25 | 1 | 55 | 86 | 255 |
|  | 25.3 | 8.8 | 0.8 | 23.4 | 0.4 | 22.0 | 39.4 | 16.0 |
| Know 2 – 4 | 120 | 108 | 115 | 48 | 51 | 178 | 83 | 703 |
|  | 47.4 | 43.2 | 43.9 | 44.9 | 20.3 | 71.2 | 38.1 | 44.2 |
| 5 plus | 10 | 113 | 141 | 10 | 198 |  | 21 | 493 |
|  | 4.0 | 45.2 | 53.8 | 9.3 | 78.9 |  | 9.6 | 31.0 |
| Column | 253 | 250 | 262 | 107 | 251 | 250 | 218 | 1591 |

Note: In Can Serra, respondents were only asked their knowledge of four groups.

general social cohesion and local opportunities, the recreational groups on their own would be unlikely to be tackling social issues or local problems in an explicit way, or to be making special efforts to involve the disadvantaged. Respondents were therefore asked whether they knew about a selection of the more prominent groups known to be active in their locality. Groups prioritised here were those with an explicit community or social issue purpose. The results are shown in **Table 2.14**.

In interpreting this picture it needs to be borne in mind the different number of groups existing in each locality, and perhaps also their longevity (see Chapter 3). In Oliveira do Douro, with relatively few groups, and those mostly recreational in their stated function but very long-lived, most people had heard of 5, 6, 7, 8 or more groups. In Thamesmead, with a large number of groups, but many of recent origin - and in a locality where many people had only arrived in recent years - only half the sample had heard of two or more groups. In Tallaght, with a large number of groups, over half the sample knew of more than five groups. It is notable that group awareness was higher in the localities in the Southern countries and Ireland.

Another interesting contrast is to see that in Perama, where groups were very little recognised or supported by the authorities, knowledge of groups was high, whilst in Ghent, where formal groups received a higher level of official support, only half had heard of two or more groups, and 23% had heard of none at all (compared with 3% in Perama).

To have heard of none of the listed groups may indicate a lack of interest

*53*

in the social issues and collective life of one's locality. In some cases this could reflect a high degree of mobility and independence, but an alarming degree of social isolation is surely the more likely explanation in most cases, given that these are areas of higher than average deprivation. Those who had heard of only one group may be not far off from isolation as well. In Thamesmead for example, for many of the 40% of the sample who had heard of only one group, the group concerned was the Citizen's Advice Bureau, a well-respected national organisation having local branches to provide a much-used service but not involving most of its users participatively. Another 13% had not even heard of the CAB.

Taking 'none' and 'only one' together, it is clear that in many localities there are likely to be substantial sections of the population who are barely involved in the social issue aspect of the life of the locality. This is most marked in Ghent, Amsterdam Mid-North and Thamesmead: the first with a substantial migrant minority and an elderly indigenous population in a declined industrial area; the last with a younger and more varied population in an area newly built over the past 25 years, and many of whom had settled there only in the past few years.

Even in localities where a majority of people had heard of several such groups, there were often still substantial minorities who had not - 11% in Perama, 29% in Can Serra. Only in Oliveira do Douro and Tallaght could one say that almost the whole population was aware of such groups, but it should be noted that the listing of groups in Oliveira do Douro leaned more to the social and recreational than other lists, because of the dearth of social issue groups in the locality, so the picture here may be overoptimistic. It is important, then, to note that even in some places where it is the norm to be aware of at least a few groups, a significant minority of people are still untouched by them. Many of these would no doubt be people who are also most isolated in other ways, and this reinforces caution against assuming that the local groups sector spontaneously reaches all disadvantaged people.

### Table 2.15
### Active on one or more issues by knowledge of groups

| Count Column % | Know none | Know one | Know 2-5 | 5 plus | Row Total |
|---|---|---|---|---|---|
| Not Active | 163 | 218 | 509 | 318 | 1208 |
|  | 86.2 | 82.3 | 78.3 | 65.2 | 75.9 |
| Active on 1+ | 26 | 47 | 141 | 170 | 384 |
|  | 13.8 | 17.7 | 21.7 | 34.8 | 24.1 |
| Column Total | 189 | 265 | 650 | 488 | 1592 |
|  | 11.9 | 16.6 | 40.8 | 30.7 | 100.0 |

## Knowledge of issue groups and level of activity

Did people's awareness of local social issue groups bear any relation to their readiness to be active on problems they had identified in the locality? **Table 2.15** throws light on this. A considerable relationship is evident. People who knew more groups were also more active on local issues, but not necessarily always through the groups. 14% of people who knew none of the groups were nevertheless active on local issues, but activity on issues seems to rise steadily with knowledge of groups. It may work either way round: becoming active leads people to find groups, or knowing about groups stimulates their activity. Probably both things are taking place. This suggests that at least part of the passivity of the majority is attributable to their unawareness of groups and of the activities undertaken by them.

Later responses (see below) show that relatively few people (11%) saw groups as a main recourse for problem-solving, so the relationship between group activity and problem-solving is not always a direct one. This makes the relationship all the more important, since the active people's form of activity was not always through the groups. The groups seem to serve a background function in either stimulating or supporting citizen activity in general, not merely through their own specific channels.

How far, then, did people make use of groups for various purposes, and were they actively involved in helping any groups? It has been seen from the examination of groups themselves that they were often run by a small core of active people - often too small, in their own view, for the work that needed doing. Those who put most in often got most out, in that participation itself was one of the main benefits, but a larger - sometimes much larger - number of people benefitted directly or indirectly from group activities. A pattern of usage and involvement can be seen whereby the groups of various kinds are clearly serving an important function for substantial sections of the population but there is no single type of group which is doing this for the majority.

## Telephones

Whilst face-to-face contact is undoubtedly the fundamental medium of local community life, modern communications technology is also important. Problems of transport, identified earlier as a major local issue, must also have been a factor facilitating or impeding local community action. A further important sidelight is thrown onto the question of social isolation by looking at the function of the **telephone** in local action. Most people in the EC have a telephone in their household, and its use is so integral to our daily way of life that we hardly think about it. However the minority who do not have access to a phone is not insignificant, and whilst it is different from country to country (Ireland for example having the largest such minority), in all countries those without a phone are also amongst those most likely to be lacking other basic facilities.

The telephone plays a vital if little-considered role in local action. A whole segment of the voluntary sector, such as confidential 'helplines' for all sorts of problems like child abuse, AIDS and despair, has grown up around the telephone. In earlier stages of this study it was found that social networks are nowadays likely to be spread selectively over a fairly wide locality rather than necessarily concentrated in the immediate neighbourhood (Chanan and Vos, pp 16ff.) In sustaining such a network it is clear that the telephone plays a fundamental role.

It is highly likely that the people without telephones are also amongst the

### Table 2.16
### Ownership of telephone by locality

| Count Column % Phone | Perama | Tallaght | Oliveira do Douro | Can Serra | Thames-mead | Row Total |
|---|---|---|---|---|---|---|
| Own phone | 198 | 191 | 189 | 237 | 173 | 988 |
|  | 79.2 | 72.9 | 75.3 | 94.8 | 79.4 | 80.3 |
| No phone | 52 | 71 | 62 | 13 | 45 | 191 |
|  | 20.8 | 27.1 | 24.7 | 5.2 | 20.6 | 15.5 |
| Column Total | 250 | 262 | 251 | 250 | 218 | 1231 |
|  | 20.3 | 21.3 | 20.4 | 20.3 | 17.7 | 100.0 |

Note: In Ghent SI & M and Amsterdam, the question about ownership of telephones was not asked.

### Table 2.17
### Activity on one or more issues by telephone ownership

|  | Phone? | | |
|---|---|---|---|
| Count Column % Activity | Own phone | No phone | Row |
| Not Active | 731 | 193 | 924 |
|  | 72.8 | 78.3 | 73.9 |
| Active 1+ | 273 | 53 | 326 |
|  | 27.2 | 21.7 | 26.1 |
| Column Total | 1004 | 246 | 1250 |
|  | 80.3 | 19.7 | 100.0 |

most isolated in other ways. Figures on telephones are available for five of the localities. The percentage of those without phones is shown in **Table 2.16**. There is some correlation between having a phone and being active on local issues (**Table 2.17**). This has to be seen in relation to the fact that few local action groups, even those dealing with problems of disadvantage, reached the whole local population, and in particular the most disadvantaged people within that population. This confirms an impression which arises from several different directions in the literature, that local action groups help alleviate disadvantage, or prevent worse disadvantage, down to a certain level and within a certain network, but do little for people who are in extreme disadvantage or isolation. This must be kept firmly in mind when considering policies which seek to ascribe responsibility for social welfare to the local action sector. However, it is often equally or even more difficult for public services to reach isolated people.

## Sources of help and levels of satisfaction

The final set of figures is a crucial one in trying to relate the function of groups to social policy, to general social cohesion and to the functions of public authorities. Here it had been asked, quite separately from general use of groups, to whom respondents turned for help with any kind of problem, and how much satisfaction they got with the response. The pattern that emerges has a similarity across most of the countries which is all the more remarkable for the fact that the countries are so different in the other ways seen above.

Overall (**Table 2.18**) **people went mainly to friends, relatives and neighbours to help them solve what they saw as personal problems, and to authorities for 'official' problems**. To a much lesser extent they went to **influential individuals** and to **local groups**. This is perhaps less surprising than the fact

**Table 2.18**

**Recourses for problems, all localities combined**

| Recourses | Count | % respond -ents |
|---|---|---|
| Local groups | 178 | 10.2 |
| Friends, relations and neighbours | 733 | 41.8 |
| Authorities | 737 | 42.1 |
| Influential people | 240 | 13.7 |

Note: Count is number of respondents using each recourse at least once, percent refers to proportion of all respondents using recourse.

## Table 2.19
## Type of recourse for problems by locality

| Count Total % | Ghent Sl & M | Perama | Tallaght | Amsterdam N | Oliveira do Douro | Can Serra | Thamesmead | Total % Total |
|---|---|---|---|---|---|---|---|---|
| Local groups | 32 | 36 | 16 | 5 | 3 | 51 | 26 | 169 |
| | 12.6 | 14.4 | 6.1 | 4.7 | 1.2 | 20.4 | 11.9 | 10.6 |
| Friends/ family/ neighbours | 87 | 142 | 87 | 92 | 43 | 95 | 60 | 606 |
| | 34.4 | 56.8 | 33.2 | 86.0 | 17.1 | 38.0 | 27.5 | 38.1 |
| Authorities | 87 | 82 | 41 | 83 | 84 | 135 | 102 | 614 |
| | 34.4 | 32.8 | 15.6 | 77.6 | 33.5 | 54.0 | 46.8 | 38.6 |
| Influential | 26 | 73 | 57 | 4 | 16 | 27 | 30 | 233 |
| | 10.3 | 29.2 | 21.8 | 3.7 | 6.4 | 10.8 | 13.8 | 15.7 |

Note: Cells contain count of number of respondents using each recourse at least once. Percent shows proportion of all respondents using each recourse.

that the pattern does not differ from one country to another as much as might have been expected (**Table 2.19**). Friends, relatives and neighbours are hardly any less important in the northern countries than the southern, so clearly the existence of an 'advanced' welfare state does not lessen the importance of personal networks. Use of authorities was also no higher in northern than southern countries, though it was particularly low in Tallaght, no doubt reflecting the weakness of local authorities there, and the communications gap between people and government agencies which is stressed in the Irish report.

Recourse to influential individuals was most important in Perama and Tallaght but also played an appreciable role in other countries, while recourse to local groups varied from almost insignificance in Oliveira do Douro to 20% of people in Can Serra.

It is clear by comparing these figures with the much higher figures for **involvement** in groups (**Table 2.9**) that people go to groups for a range of other purposes than in order to solve a specific problem. This made sense in terms of examination of how groups work. If they are successfully meeting a need they are not necessarily described as 'solving a problem'; but in the broader sense their activities clearly are part of the solution to what would otherwise be problems, such as a lack of facilities, lack of social contacts, activities and networks.

People were also asked how satisfied they were with help received from these four sources when they did go to them in connection with problems. Here the responses show an even more remarkable convergence (**Tables 2.20, 2.21, 2.22 and 2.23**). Generally, **satisfaction with friends, relatives and neighbours was high; satisfaction with authorities was low or medium; satisfaction with influential people was medium; satisfaction**

**with groups was high.**

Illustration from the national studies again adds depth to this picture, on such matters as the relative importance of friends, relatives and neighbours, on the different types of problem which led people to look for help from authorities or from personal networks, and on the remarkably widespread phenomenon that few people went to groups for help with problems yet those that did got high satisfaction.

### Table 2.20
### Satisfaction with different recourses for problems by locality: Local groups and oganisations

| % | Ghent SI & M | Perama | Tallaght | Amster-dam N | Oliveira do Douro | Can Serra | Thames-mead | Total |
|---|---|---|---|---|---|---|---|---|
| Very helpful | 61 | 36 | 75 | | | 51 | 80 | 97 54.8 |
| Quite helpful | 28 | 31 | 10 | 25 | 33 | 25 | 12 | 41 23.1 |
| Not helpful | 11 | 33 | 15 | 75 | 66 | 25 | 8 | 39 22.0 |
| No of respond-ents | 36 | 36 | 20 | 4 | 3 | 53 | 25 | 177 |

Note: Cells show proportion of respondents satisfied using each recourse.

### Table 2.21
### Satisfaction with different recourses for problems by locality: Friends, relations and neighbours

| % | Ghent SI & M | Perama | Tallaght | Amster-dam N | Oliveira do Douro | Can Serra | Thames-mead | Total |
|---|---|---|---|---|---|---|---|---|
| Very helpful | 72 | 13 | 81 | 73 | 56 | 88 | 88 | 402 63.8 |
| Quite helpful | 18 | 33 | 14 | 13 | 27 | 5 | 8 | 112 17.8 |
| Not helpful | 11 | 55 | 5 | 14 | 16 | 6 | 3 | 117 18.4 |
| No of respond-ents | 85 | 141 | 152 | 56 | 44 | 93 | 60 | 631 |

Note: Cells show proportion of respondents satisfied using each recourse.

**Table 2.22**
**Satisfaction with different recourses for problems by locality: Public authorities**

| % | Ghent SI & M | Perama | Tallaght | Amsterdam N | Oliveira do Douro | Can Serra | Thamesmead | Total |
|---|---|---|---|---|---|---|---|---|
| Very helpful | 51 | 32 | 31 | 64 | 44 | 30 | 19 | 247 38.8 |
| Quite helpful | 14 | 21 | 26 | 9 | 19 | 15 | 37 | 124 19.5 |
| Not helpful | 35 | 48 | 43 | 27 | 39 | 55 | 44 | 266 41.8 |
| No of respondents | 97 | 82 | 42 | 102 | 86 | 122 | 106 | 637 |

Note: Cells show proportion of respondents satisfied using each recourse.

**Table 2.23**
**Satisfaction with different recourses for problems by locality: Influential people**

| % | Ghent SI & M | Perama | Tallaght | Amsterdam N | Oliveira do Douro | Can Serra | Thamesmead | Total |
|---|---|---|---|---|---|---|---|---|
| Very helpful | 44 | 19 | 61 | 100 | 41 | 36 | 45 | 96 40.2 |
| Quite helpful | 12 | 25 | 12 | - | 29 | 7 | 38 | 47 19.8 |
| Not helpful | 44 | 56 | 27 | - | 29 | 57 | 17 | 95 40.0 |
| No. of respondents | 25 | 72 | 66 | 1 | 17 | 28 | 29 | 238 |

A high use of neighbours was characteristic of respondents in **Oliveira do Douro** (more than 50% of the 'friends/relatives/neighbours' group). 'This points to the existence of neighbourhood solidarity networks which are used as a means of coping with the inadequacy of State social provision' (P,60).

In **Can Serra** a clear difference could be detected in the types of problem for which people had recourse to different sources of help. As far as the local groups and associations were concerned, interviewees said they were chiefly looking for advice or counselling, often about housing or education.

In approaching official organisations, they were generally seeking solutions to problems or complaints, mainly on employment, health and environment. Also many bureaucratic applications were included among the contacts with official bodies, such as applications for grants. In contacting neighbours, friends and relatives, the problems were of a personal character such as domestic jobs, loans, child minding, and health and housing problems were prominent.

This is interpreted as reflecting a sophisticated understanding by people of what they can expect from each other: 'The data seem to confirm that human relations themselves define the limits of the requests that can and cannot be made to the family, friends and others, with the result that a high level of efficiency in the attainment of objectives is achieved. In some cases, informal networks solve problems of major importance, eg an introduction to a company to find work, or obtaining care when one is sick, and they are able to probe areas not accessible to groups or institutions, eg first-hand information about the quality of a school ... Women are more likely than men (45% to 31%) to have recourse to informal relationships of this kind' (S,51).

Echoes of this pattern can be found in other studies, such as that in **Thamesmead**: 'Problems taken to the authorities were overwhelmingly concerned with housing issues. The next largest group concerned crime, and another concerned the local environment including such things as broken lifts and street lighting ... Problems taken to friends, relatives and neighbours were mainly to do with health, child-minding and domestic issues' (U,5.8).

Here, however, there was much less reliance on neighbours. Recourse among personal networks was mainly to relatives, both immediate family and more distant, about a third outside the locality; about 20% of such recourses were to friends and less than 10% were to neighbours. Local groups were least used, but showed variety: 'The largest category was advice groups - the Citizens' Advice Bureau, a law centre and marriage guidance centre. Others were to neighbourhood or community groups: a campaigning organisation against the poll tax, a mothers' group, a general neighbourhood group, the local wildlife group, a religious body, a trade union, a political party, sports group, social group and a campaign to impove education' (U,5.9).

In **Amsterdam Mid-North** the 40% who went to friends, relatives or neighbours mainly did so in connection with odd jobs about the house, moving, personal problems or when ill or handicapped. About 20% of women and 30% of men had made use of neighbours' help during the past year.

In **Sluizeken/Muide,** 38% of respondents had called upon friends, neighbours or relatives for assistance within the past year. Neighbours were the most called upon (64% of those in this category), friends the next most often

(38%) and relatives least (28%). Men called more on friends, women more on neighbours and relatives. Respondents of Turkish origin turned to relatives and family more often than did those of Belgian origin. The 34% of respondents who had called on official services had done so for a wide range of problems: employment, administration, health, housing, environment, racial conflict.

'There is no doubt that respondents preferred informal networks, primarily help from neighbours, in dealing with problems, and that there was a high level of satisfaction with the assistance provided. The use of official services came in second place, with rather less satisfaction at the service provided. Considerably less call was made on local groups/organisations and influential people. Nevethless there was a large difference in satisfaction. The satisfaction of the respondents who used local groups/organisations was actually slightly higher than that for informal assistance. Only 6% said they had not been helped. This was in contrast to those who called on influential people, where more said they had not been helped than had' (B, 3.17).

The same story emerged in **Tallaght**. 'Although few people used local groups and organisations to solve problems, these, in sharp contrast to state services, were rated as highly in terms of helpfulness as the more personal networks. The in-depth interviews with users... indicate the personal empathy which groups can offer, in contrast to the more impersonal approach of state agencies' (I,80).

The Irish study interpreted this as meaning that local groups and organisations occupy a special space between the state and people's personal networks, not substituting for the support of friends, neighbours or relations but providing 'a new domain of support for people'. This is illustrated in quotations from local people which are both graphic and moving:

> "'There's a big difference between going into the Centre here for information and going straight to the Department. For one thing the Centre is here in Tallaght. If I want to talk to someone in the Department I either have to go into town or I've to ring - and you know what the phones and buses are like. But the main thing is, when you go to the Centre they know where you're at. They're not going to suggest you do stupid things like going to six other state buildings to get what you want. They're not going to make you feel stupid if you don't know exactly how to say what you want to say. And they often have better information than whoever it is you'd end up talking to in the department.'"
>
> "'I have very good neighbours, I have very good friends and I have a very good family. But they were people who knew me too well. I found that when I lost my mum they would sort of shy away, they couldn't face me, they

didn't know what to expect. They didn't want to discuss my mum. I wanted to talk about her, they would change the subject. But when I came here I could speak about her. They were total strangers who never knew the woman, so I could tell them what she was like. The neighbours were inclined to cry with me. That was the last thing I wanted.'" (I,87).

Taking together what was discovered about the size of groups, their difficulties in surviving and their poor and insecure funding (see subsequent chapters), and the fact that some local people did not know about them, furnishes a conclusion which goes some way to explain the paradox that groups are performing vital public functions yet are almost invisible in public discourse: specific groups are highly valued by those who know about and use them, but many groups are too small or marginal to fulfill their potential for the majority of the local population. Mostly, they are not high-profile problem-solvers, but largely work behind the scenes, knitting together local society in unseen ways. They have a stimulating effect on local action beyond their own specific activities, but there are significant sections of local people that they do not reach, and even many of those who are involved in them probably do not realise their problem-solving potential. To sum up the condition of local groups one could say: they have a crucial role, relied on by society far more than society realises, but held back below their potential by underdevelopment, low profile and lack of resources.

## Technical note on the household questionnaire

Although the questionnaires used were broadly the same, in some localities particular questions were modified or omitted from the agreed core, to better reflect local circumstances. Thus a particular locality will not be represented in some tables. This particularly affects the following tables:
- 2.2, 2.3 and 2.4 where the Irish data on problems in the locality took a different form;
- 2.3 where unprompted issues were not recorded in the Netherlands;
- in all tables showing breakdown by age, where data from Spain are not available;
- those showing the ownership of telephones, which was not recorded in Belgium or the Netherlands.

In most tables, cells show the count and column percentage, based on all repondents. This varies in some cases. Cell contents are indicated in the top left hand corner of tables.
Statistical tests of significance are not shown here, but are considered in a separate report on more extensive re-analysis of the data which is in preparation.

# Chapter three
# Local groups: what they do

## Introduction

This chapter presents a picture of the range of activities carried out by local community groups. First it discusses **background factors** such as the relation between groups and local community action as a whole. Secondly, it looks at the **method** of collecting information, and provides an **overview of the local groups sector** in each of the case-study localities: the numbers of groups found and approached, and how many responded, together with simplified information on how autonomous they were, whether they operated mainly in the locality alone or also beyond; and how long they had been in existence (**Tables 3.1 and 3.2**). Thirdly, groups are looked at more closely. Information is given on **selected groups** which were analysed in greater depth, and their activities and achievements, with some detailed examples. Finally three aspects of **participation** in local group life are considered: people who are **excluded** from participation for one reason or another; the role of **women**; and participation by **minority ethnic** groups. How groups function is examined in the subsequent chapter, with discussion on interpretative questions such as how 'autonomy' was understood.

## Local groups and local action

The investigation of local groups and organisations was inevitably more reliant on those that were stable, visible and formal enough to be located and studied. As far as local community action as a whole is concerned, it was clear from the household survey that these were likely to be only the tip of the iceberg: people were active at many other levels, whether individually, through personal networks of friends, neighbours or relatives, or by approaching public authorities or influential individuals.

The research also enabled us to glean a certain amount of historical information on groups that had come and gone. For example there was an upsurge of local groups and popular movements in Portugal around the 1974 revolution but many folded and disappeared soon after (P,74). It was also found that many existing groups were having a hard time surviving, and even in the short period of our research we saw some groups being formed and others on the point of collapse. So our 'snapshots' are part of a **continually changing sector**.

From the household survey and other information it is also clear that there are many informal networks of friends, relatives and neighbours which carry out interactive functions but which never formalise themselves into named groups. This informal part of local action, which no doubt fluctuates according to a variety of conditions, is undoubtedly in most conditions likely to be much larger and more continuous than the life of groups, and whilst it was beyond the scope of the research to study it directly, information both from groups and households provides many insights into it which are drawn upon in the text.

Furthermore, there is another crucial aspect to the local action phenomenon which is public and visible but only in short bursts:

> 'There is a tradition of informal and ad hoc forms of action which from time to time mobilise those people who are more aware of a problem or those who are directly involved, the object being to formulate a demand to the competent authorities or... to solve it directly. Such examples abound in the history of Perama, and by way of illustration we might mention the blockading of the single road out of Perama, with the aim of drawing attention to the traffic problem and demanding the construction of a second road, or the creation of facilities for children following the initiative taken by the residents of one neighbourhood... In one way or another they give rise to a social dynamism which fuels the actions of the associations even though they are not given any organised and permanent expression' (G,119).

In studying identifiable local groups, then, it is not intended to give the impression that these are the limits of local action. They are, however, a point where local action often becomes **more articulated, more visible and more sustained**. They are also, for that reason, a point with which policy-makers can seek to interact. In some cases the authorities are keen to ascribe significant policy functions to them and it is important to study them in order to assess whether such hopes are realistic and justified. There is therefore a *de facto* importance to these kinds of groups which makes them worth studying both for their own sake and as a prism to glimpse the larger hidden realities of informal collective action.

## Method

In each locality the researchers first drew up a list of all the local groups and organisations that could be found. They then focussed on those which apparently had some social purpose relevant to public policy, leaving aside many which appeared to be devoted to social or recreational purposes of a specific and limited kind. This included a number of sports, recreation, religious and youth organisations, and branches of political parties were also eliminated. A degree of local discretion was used to decide these exclusions. They were not made without some doubts, but the aim was to focus particularly on groups which had more explicit social policy purposes. In fact, what was learnt from the groups that were studied suggests that **all local groups tend to carry out some important social functions** over and above their stated purposes. Within the samples, however, there was no shortage of groups which also carried out sports or cultural functions as part of a social policy purpose. It is also arguable that branches of political parties are *particularly* relevant. This is considered later. One thing that was clear overall was that, at local level, local action was a phenomenon quite distinct from the programmes of political parties.

The numbers of groups in the case-studies are summarised in **Table 3.1**, and combined totals are given in **Table 3.2**. The groups judged to be relevant were surveyed in some detail. The researchers investigated what they were about, how many people were involved actively, how many others were members or used their services, and how they functioned. For example, was it a self-created and self-governing group of local residents; or the branch of a national or regional voluntary organisation; or a group that had been set up by and was accountable to the local authority or some other major institution such as a church, political party or trade union? Because of different national characteristics, these categories did not apply in the same way in each locality, so the generalisations must be treated with caution. In Belgium, for example, local participatory groups are nearly always led by one or two paid workers who have secured sufficient public funding for this role, so there it is inaccurate to speak of an entirely voluntary or resident-led group.

The researchers went on in each case to select four or five groups to study in more detail, interviewing some of the key activists and some regular users about their views on the role, achievements and problems of the organisations.

## Emerging contours of local groups sectors

The varied character of local groups begins to emerge from these profiles. The largest numbers of groups were found in Tallaght and Amsterdam Mid-North. This did not mean that the largest proportions of local people were necessarily involved. The largest extent of active involvement was probably in Tallaght. The smallest number of groups was found in Oliveira do Douro but the largest proportion of people in the locality were members of those groups; yet, again, what those groups did in terms of social policy was in some ways very constrained.

In some places the groups were very much aware of each other and formed **wide networks** among themselves. In others the relationships were

## Table 3.1
## Locality studies: summary profiles of local groups sector
For terminology see section on 'Definitions' in chapter one.
Some figures are approximate due to simplification for comparative purposes.

---

**Belgium: SLUIZEKEN AND MUIDE (Ghent)**
*Population:* 12,250
46 groups found and approached, 40 responded, 28 judged relevant.
*Control\*:*
6 autonomous groups, 14 semi-autonomous, 8 externally-led.
*Territory:*
most operated in the locality or beyond.
*Duration:*
13 created in past 5 years, 13 5 - 15 years ago, 2 over 15 years.

---

\* Most local groups in Sluizeken/Muide were 'private', ie. led by professionals enlisting volunteers. These groups were also often affiliated to national organisations. In this summary they are therefore listed as semi-autonomous.

---

**Greece: PERAMA (Athens)**
*Population:* 30,000
58 groups found, 30 judged relevant and approached, 27 responded.
*Control:*
15 autonomous groups, 9 semi-autonomous, 3 externally-led.
*Territory:*
most operated in locality.
*Duration:*
17 created in past 7 years, 14 7-16 years ago.

---

**Ireland: TALLAGHT (Dublin)**
*Population:* 80,000
200+ groups found, 117 judged relevant and approached, 61 responded.
*Control:*
34 autonomous groups, 15 semi-autonomous, 12 externally-led.
*Territory:*
22 operated across whole locality, 39 in part.
*Duration:*
16 created in past 5 years, 26 5-10 years ago, 17 more than 10.

**Portugal: OLIVEIRA DO DOURO (Oporto)**
*Population:* 32,000
31 groups found and approached, 29 responded.
*Control:*
22 autonomous, 7 externally-led.
*Territory:* 25 operated in locality, 4 also beyond.
*Duration:* 5 groups created in past 16 years, 24 over 16 years ago (end of dictatorship).

**Netherlands: AMSTERDAM MID-NORTH (Amsterdam)**
*Population:* 32,000
200+ groups found, 143 judged relevant and approached, 92 responded.
*Control:*
58 autonomous groups, 10 semi-autonomous, 24 externally-led.
*Territory:*
46 operated in locality only, 46 also beyond.
*Duration:*
22 created in past 3 years, 32 3-10 years ago, 38 more than 10.

**Spain: CAN SERRA (Barcelona)**
*Population:* 13,000
67 groups found, 47 judged relevant and approached, 32 responded.
*Control:*
17 autonomous groups, 9 semi-autonomous, 6 externally-led.
*Territory:*
24 operated in locality, 9 also beyond.
*Duration:* most groups created 10-20 years ago.

**UK: THAMESMEAD (London)**
*Population:* 28,500
91 groups found, 51 judged relevant and approached, 32 responded.
*Control:*
15 autonomous groups, 11 semi-autonomous, 6 externally-led.
*Territory:*
28 groups operated in locality, 14 outside.
*Duration:* 19 groups created in past 3 years, 20 3-12 years ago, 20 over 12.

**Table 3.2**
**Local groups sectors: combined figures from the seven localities**

| | | |
|---|---|---|
| Total groups found | 693 | |
| approached | 465 | |
| responded | 313 | |
| response rate | 67% | |
| | | |
| **Control** | | |
| Information available on | 301 groups | |
| autonomous | 167 | 55% |
| semi-autonomous | 68 | 23% |
| externally-led | 66 | 22% |

'molecular' and many groups knew only a few others and were not aware of the overall picture. In some places the public authorities were funding most of the groups, for example three quarters of them in Amsterdam Mid-North, in others only a handful; in Oliveira do Douro and Perama the local authority was providing a flat rate grant to all recognised groups - but the flat rate was very low, and the criteria for recognition as a group could be very rigid. In Thamesmead, variation in public funding to groups was acute, from a few receiving sufficient funding to employ several staff full time, to others getting a little and most getting nothing.

Despite these variations, four features justify speaking of the groups as the visible part of a **local community action sector** which was both distinct in each locality and comparable across the localities in different countries:
a  there was always some **networking** between groups;
b  there was often some form of official or unofficial **umbrella group** supporting a range of groups;
c  its importance and its existence as a sector **distinct from ordinary public services** was recognised by most local people and policy makers; and
d  most decisively, as will appear from the more detailed material, many of the functions, achievements and problems of groups had profound **underlying similarities** of a quite different nature from those of either established public institutions, commercial businesses or individual households.

Despite many national differences, the pattern of local group life is too similar to be accidental. All seven case study areas proved to have not merely a few groups but **a range of groups of different kinds tackling similar issues**. This is also implicitly corroborated by a number of other studies both in the case-study countries and elsewhere, though it is remarkable how many studies in this field *assume* the existence of a wide range of groups and refer to them obliquely without ever profiling the groups in a given locality.

Another common point is the variable contribution of internal and external factors to the existence of groups. All countries had some sort of national voluntary sector, which in many cases initiated or supported action in a number of localities; all local authorities had some sort of policy towards use of or support for local groups; some governments and regional authorities had taken special initiatives in relation to selected localities over and above their universal administrative measures. But the variations are complex. The ways in which groups could become legitimated and get access to funding and support were very varied, but groups in all localities seemed to be **chronically underfunded** for the job they were trying to do.

In most cases, the particular configuration of groups bore **no predetermined relation to particular social issues** but rather a variety of contingent factors went to make one kind of group more viable than another. National traditions play an important role here. Each country has one or more areas of social policy where the role of local groups has more or less established itself and gained recognition, whilst other areas of policy, which are equally important, are hardly recognised or are not reflected in local groups. However, underlying these differences is a clear tendency of groups, once established, to play a **general socially cohesive** role beyond the specific issue that gave rise to the group.

## 'Focus' groups and policy issues

A list of the selected 'focus groups' studied in depth in each locality is given in **Table 3.3**. These of course were only a fraction of the groups in the locality. They were selected with some attention to their relevance to the pre-identified policy issues. Taking account both of these and of the overall trawl of groups, the following observations suggest how the groups related to the pre-identified policy issues. The relation of groups to policy in general is examined in chapter five.

### Unemployment

This was not frequently addressed by groups as a distinct issue separate from its **effects**, which more often appeared under headings like health, housing, homelessness, or attempts to **overcome** unemployment, which showed up more often under 'training'. Two major exceptions, however, were the Tallaght Centre for the Unemployed and the Unemployed Shipyard Workers' Organisation and BAANderij, in Amsterdam Mid-North.

### Health

The Netherlands' model of 'patients' societies' with an explicit all-round health role (as in Bannedok) was exceptional. More typical for other countries were fairly specialist organisations like Can Serra's Association for Aiding the Mentally Handicapped. Many health issues were being addressed in other ways, such as Tallaght's 'Helping Hands' organisation for people caring for children with disabilities, or Thamesmead's 'Meet A Mum' for

## Table 3.3
## Groups selected for in-depth study

### Sluizeken and Muide (Belgium)
1 The Jam Club Youth Centre
2 The Thuishaven Social Centre
3 Steunpunt Gent Community Development (OSG) Sluizeken Residents' and Steering Committees
4 De Poort-Beraber Integration Centre

### Perama (Greece)
1 Cultural Centre
2 Parent Teacher Association (sixth primary school)
3 Ikaros (planning and environment)
4 Women's House

### Tallaght (Ireland)
1 Helping Hands (families of disabled children)
2 Tallaght Adult and Community Training (TACT)
3 Tallaght Women's Contact Centre (TWCC)
4 Tallaght Centre for the Unemployed (TCU)

### Amsterdam Mid-North (Netherlands)
1 Bannedok Patients' Society
2 Vogelbuurt and IJ-Plein Working Group
3 Moroccan Culture Group (AMG)
4 Unemployed Shipyard Workers' Organisation and BAANderij

### Oliveira do Douro (Portugal)
1 Olveira do Douro Community Association (APOD)
2 Drama and Recreation Group
3 Culture and Leisure Association
4 Mutual Aid Association
5 Secondary School Parent-Teacher Association

### Can Serra (Spain)
1 Can Serra Residents' Association
2 Can Serra Pensioners' Association
3 Culture Promotion Group of Torras i Bages Institute
4 Association for Aiding the Mentally Handicapped

### Thamesmead (United Kingdom)
1 Trust Thamesmead (umbrella group)
2 Meet a Mum Association
3 Binsey Walk Tenants' Association
4 The Archway Project (education/unemployment)
5 Thamesmead Wildlife Trust

women suffering post-natal depression. Health was a major underlying issue in many groups, closely associated with women's role.

**Education and training**
Training, we have said, was associated with measures to overcome unemployment, and was a major focus of a number of groups. Education as a general issue was again a major underlying aspect of local groups, and again mainly associated with women's role. Parent-teacher associations in Perama had a wide-ranging local approach not limited to the functions of schools. A similar centrality for parents' associations could be found in Can Serra and in background material from Italy (Giaconi and Vitali, 1990).

**The environment, including built environment**
Whilst there were relatively few groups at local level which identified themselves by name as 'environmentalist', like Thamesmead's Wildlife Trust or Perama's 'Ikaros', environmental issues were of widespread concern to other groups, particularly generalist local organisations dealing with the physical conditions of the locality, such as Amsterdam North's Vogelbuurt and IJ-Plein Working Group. In Can Serra, the existence of compulsory 'block associations', whereby residents of a block of flats were jointly responsible for certain collective functions, was an important legitimating factor for those types of group, which often took on more issues than they were statutorily obliged to.

A clear message from the household survey and groups is that there is a **huge concern with environment** which is not reflected adequately in specific groups. This is an issue - **transport** is another - which has to be taken up at a higher level. There are indeed a variety of well-known and effective environmental organisations operating at national and international levels. There are some important findings here for those organisations. The **local aspects of environment are often not being adequately taken up**, and the national organisations, like other national voluntary organisations, often look on their local branches only as supporters of the national initiatives, not as semi-autonomous groups who also need to take local action, for which they need support, advice and expertise from the centre or from each other. It seems probable that national environmental organisations are missing enormous opportunities and responsibilities to link their national positions with specific local dimensions that people want to tackle.

By implication this issue also covers **planning**, which requires specific comment. One of the most fundamental changes with which people were coping in several of the case-study localities (and which is endemic in contemporary European development) was **rapid urbanisation.** With innumerable examples of local action generated by the need for basic facilities and amenities, a major overall finding of the study must be that planning methods, whether by authorities or by operation of the free market, **do not on their own result in liveable habitations**. There is an essential complementary role for local resident organisations at all stages in the physical growth of a locality. This is universally treated in a reactive way - something that people may take up late in the day, when new estates, planned or accumulated, turn out to be dreadful living environments. The wastefulness and social aggravation of this 'system' is staggering. It seems to be necessary for people to be placed in bad conditions in order to react to them before planners and other authorities appear to be capable of assessing what conditions and amenities would make life there tolerable.

This is an area where the **social partners**, particularly in the form of property and development companies may have a major role to play, and, exceptionally, there is evidence that some companies are developing new practices in this direction.

### Transport

Even fewer were the groups specifically dedicated to the issue of transport, indeed it was hard to find any *long-term* groups at local level for whom this was the main focus; but again it was an issue of **widespread concern**, reflected in the activities of a variety of generalist and other groups. The predicament of the locality determined whether mobility or congestion was the uppermost problem, but in either case there was an evident **difficulty in tackling the issue from a local base**. Apart from the physical fact of needing to transcend the local scale, participation seemed to be particularly impeded by the remoteness of the relevant authorities and their apparent lack of any institutional culture of seeking to relate to community groups, such as was found in areas like health, education and housing for at least several countries.

### Women

The crucial role of women has emerged in many different ways and is discussed later in this chapter.

## Examples of achievements

The achievements of local groups are often hidden. This is because they happen to different people in different ways and at different times, and in aggregate are known only to small numbers of people. Many achievements are small-scale and only gain wider significance in their cumulative effect. Even vital achievements, such as **acquiring new amenities for the locality, monitoring public services or providing help to people in distress** are often either not known to the general public or not known to have been achieved by local community action.

Evaluation of local action, if it exists at all, is spasmodic; but the following are some indications of the kinds of thing which local groups were achieving, from the locality case studies.

As part of the study in **Amsterdam Mid-North** (Netherlands), 82 groups reviewed the effects of their activity over the preceding two years. 51 were satisfied or very satisfied that they had achieved worthwhile results. Some had been externally evaluated. Part of the work of the Vogelburt and IJ Plein Working Group - a joint resident/local council forum originally begun by residents - had been formally evaluated in 1989, after two years' action, by independent researchers commissioned by the local authority. The researchers, residents and district councillors all agreed that the approach had brought a **definite improvement to local quality of life**.

In **Sluizeken and Muide** (Belgium), similarly, most groups felt they had achieved practical results. Some had provided **language lessons, training and personal help**. One group had achieved the rearrangement of a public area to create **better road safety**. Others saw their effect in mobilising self-help: 'Users have been activated to give spontaneous mutual help' (B, 4.6). The 'Jam Club', a youth group, was used by about 100 people aged 14 to 20, many of them coming several times a week. Young people of different ethnic groups mixed, took responsibility for organising activities themselves, and were drawn into activities for the benefit of the neighbourhood as a whole such as campaigns for better living conditions and 'child-friendly streets'. This in turn drew adults into community activity: 'It has become clear that the youth centre... motivates residents to take part in discussions and campaigns concerning the future of the area... Both the youth and the other residents know that they can bring such matters to the youth club and that some effective action will be organised' (B, 4.13).

In the localities in the Southern countries and in Tallaght the achievements of local action were in some ways more popularly understood. This may have been because the limitations of the public services were clearer; no doubt in the case of Greece, Portugal and Spain it was also because of the political sensitisation accompanying the revolutionary changes of the mid seventies. Yet the detailed effects were sometimes just as dispersed and hidden from general public acknowledgement.

Local action had had a formative influence in the development of **Can Serra** (Spain) between 1970 and 80, spanning the transition from dictatorship to democracy. Working through social pressure groups at the time when overt political groups were prohibited, residents in this newly-built area put the brakes on speculative building, got rid of a factory that was causing pollution and secured basic amenities, such as paved roads and public open spaces - 'In the 1970's, things got done!' (S,54). With the transition to democracy, some of the momentum of local action was transferred into the political process, so that the area has a high level of political and trade union membership, voting turnout and general membership of associations, but the focus of local action groups has shifted from pressure and campaigning towards lower-profile activity dealing with social problems, especially education and health. Nevertheless negotiating for physical improvement of the area continues - the most recent achievement being an underground car park, covered by a garden, to reduce congestion and danger and add an outdoor facility.

**Joint action and socialising re-inforce each other: local men construct a bowls park over the underground car park for which residents ran a successful campaign in Can Serra (Spain). Women played a prominent part in the campaign.**

**Tallaght** (Ireland) was the case study which showed most active involvement of people in local groups: 'The services and activities of groups were rated very highly, and there was an acceptance of the "normality" of involvement in such groups' (I,115).

**Oliveira do Douro** (Portugal), however, had the largest number of people in membership of groups; the autonomous associations had a fundamental role in ensuring social cohesion, though not in addressing overt social issues: 'Groups tend to represent an opportunity for general conviviality and leisure, a means of strengthening people's sense of being part of a community, with all its traditions and customs - that is the role that makes them so dear to the local population ... Rare is the citizen of Oliveira do Douro who is not a member of at least two groups' (P,76-8).

**Perama** (Greece) displayed a stress on action taking place outside groups, but this was by no means instead of group activity - it was, rather, something which interacted with it: 'The role of the local associations and of the municipal agencies at local level is exceptionally important for the local community and for the organisation and mobilisation of that community in order to cope with problems... They have a very important role as leaders and catalysts in the organisation, mobilisation, counselling and informing of local people and, at the same time, they are in a position to offer a wide spectrum of services in direct contact with the needs and problems of the residents' (G, 8.8-9).

Caring never stops: children with special needs are taken to see the opening of the Christmas lights in Tallaght town centre (Ireland) by a local carers' groups, 'Helping Hands'.

## Quantification

Can these kinds of achievement be put in terms of numbers? To some extent yes, though little quantitative evaluation in this field has been carried out in the past. With what is now known, through this and other recent studies, it would be possible, and worthwhile, to devise a systematic way of quantifying the benefits, distinguishing the various levels of benefit which emerge in the present discussion. From some of our existing material we can already illustrate the scale of activities:

> 'Each of the four (intensively studied) groups provide services to relatively large numbers of people. Up to 800 women visit the Women's Centre each week, approximately 1500 people use the Tallaght Centre for the Unemployed on an annual basis, 400 people a year sign up for Tallaght Adult and Community Training courses, and Helping Hands has 40 regular users and contact with 150 others' (I, 120).

> 'The Thuishaven (social centre for the over-55s) was used by some 500 elderly people, a large proportion of whom lived in the flats above the Centre... The majority were over 65's or over 70's living on a small pension ... The Centre had succeeded in giving a considerable number of them the opportunity to remain living in their

own homes, in providing them with meaningful ways to spend their time, protecting them fom loneliness and in promoting mutual solidarity through informal mutual assistance' (B, 4.19-22).

'The School for Adults endeavours to act as a driving force within the neighbourhood and to integrate the underprivileged by means of education... The main study areas are general elementary education, vocational training and cultural activities. During the past year 400 people took part... 80% of the students can be classified as regular participants' (S,72-3).

However, benefits cannot be *reduced* to numbers. One cannot easily weigh intense benefit received by a few people against incidental benefit received by many - though this is in fact a common difference between groups:

'Of the 61 Tallaght groups, 47 were providing services to their communities... These vary considerably in terms of the numbers less than 25 people used their services over the past twelve months, 8 reported between 25 and 50, 8 indicated between 50 and 100, 14 between 100 and 500 and eleven groups indicated over 500. Groups providing services to large numbers are mainly those which provide information or some related service on a drop-in basis. Small numbers indicate more intensive services such as counselling, training, personal development... The more personalised and intensive the service, the fewer will be the numbers availing of it at any one time' (I,97,120).

## Complex effects

The complexity of the effects which a local organisation can pursue is well illustrated by one of the Dutch groups, the Bannedok Patients' Society. This group's first achievement was to get a health centre set up for the neighbourhood. Eventually this led to the creation of a society carrying out a whole spider's web of functions for the locality:

'When Banne-Nord was completed in the seventies there were few facilities, and those there were, were not properly housed. Dissatisfaction with the way the one-man practice GPs, social workers and other carers was organised was a further reason for the residents to try to get a number of facilities housed under one roof... A group of residents started work to have a health centre built' (N, 139)

When, after a long struggle, the Centre was established, the residents remained involved, making sure the facility was user-friendly and that it would maintain a broad range of disciplines. In 1983 the campaigning group turned itself into a formal society, and became an indispensable channel by which the Centre, now run by the authorities, consulted with local residents. From this base, the society became involved in the health aspect of a whole range of local issues and agencies (See **Table 3.4**)

There are some 1,500 families registered at the health centre. About 250 are members of the Patients' Society, paying a small annual subscription. The active work of the society is done by a six-member executive team, five of whom are women, helped by a fluctuating number of active members: 'Together with the team members, the active members of the society sit on a number of ad hoc committees. There is a newsletter committee, a publicity committee, a committee to discuss residents' complaints and a reporting committee which carefully records any health matters reported in Banne-Buiksloot and, where necessary, informs other bodies of these matters' (N,142). The society also contributes to city-wide networks and campaigns.

The work of the society clearly brings **benefits to the entire locality and beyond, in multiple ways**. The 1,500 Centre-using families get particular benefits, including the quarterly newsletter 'Better Banne', which gives practical advice on health and increases the involvement of users: 'The active members feel the newsletter helps to reduce the distance between patient and carer and lowers the threshold for some people to come to the Centre with a problem' (N,145). The 250 members presumably feel they are helping the society to run, and within them the executive and the few dozen activists - never enough, they say - are the doers and decision-makers. They are also channels of stimulus and information in many small, invisible ways: 'Even outside the neighbourhood, your relatives as well... Whatever information you get from the health centre, you naturally pass it on. I do this quite consciously...' (N, 144).

Another example of many-sided effects emanating from a key local organisation comes from Italy, where a special report gathered background material for this study (Giaconi and Vitali, 1990). The 'Proletarian Culture Centre' in the Magliana District (Lazio region) near Rome was a response to rapid, uncontrolled urbanisation similar to several of the case-studies in this research:

> 'An unhealthy district, in a damp and foggy area, dangerous on account of the lack of reliable boundaries for the river Tiber, unsuitable for building because of the different levels of the river bank and the surrounding countryside, was the area in which, during the 1970s, in contravention of planning laws and technical recommendations, housing was constructed for 38,000 people... Another problem was the sewers, which flowed

**Table 3.4**
**The role of the Patients' Society both in Bannedok and outside it**

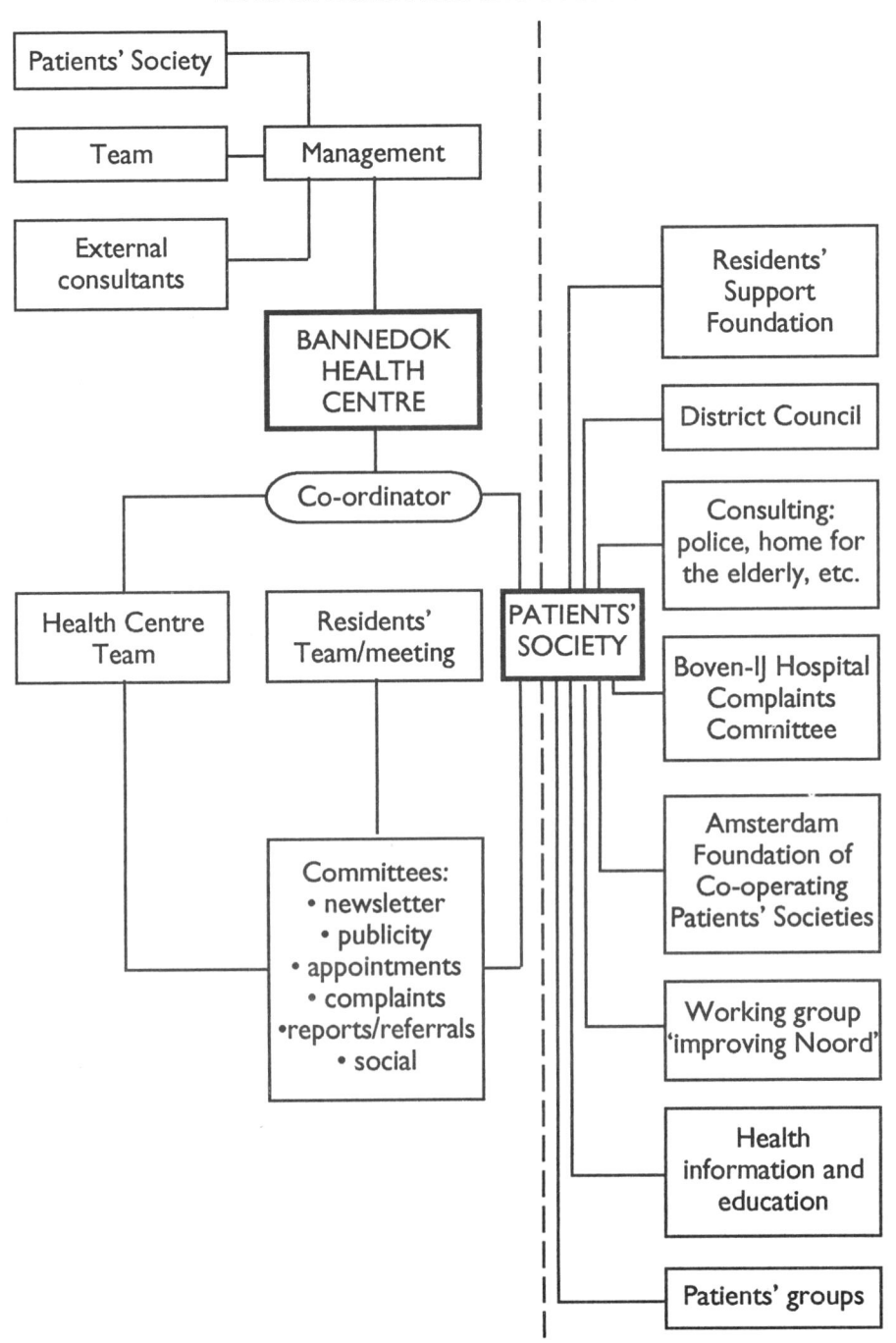

```
┌──────────────────┐
│ Patients' Society│──┐
└──────────────────┘  │
┌──────────────────┐  │                              ┌──────────────┐
│      Team        │─┤Management│                    │  Residents'  │
└──────────────────┘  │                              │   Support    │
┌──────────────────┐  │                              │  Foundation  │
│    External      │──┘                              └──────────────┘
│   consultants    │
└──────────────────┘                                 ┌──────────────┐
        ┌─────────────┐                              │District Council│
        │  BANNEDOK   │                              └──────────────┘
        │   HEALTH    │
        │   CENTRE    │                              ┌──────────────┐
        └─────────────┘                              │  Consulting: │
              │                                      │ police, home for│
        ( Co-ordinator )                             │ the elderly, etc.│
         │           │                               └──────────────┘
┌──────────────┐ ┌──────────────┐  ┌─────────┐       ┌──────────────┐
│Health Centre │ │  Residents'  │  │PATIENTS'│       │Boven-IJ Hospital│
│    Team      │ │ Team/meeting │  │ SOCIETY │       │  Complaints  │
└──────────────┘ └──────────────┘  └─────────┘       │  Committee   │
                                                     └──────────────┘
                 ┌──────────────┐                    ┌──────────────┐
                 │ Committees:  │                    │  Amsterdam   │
                 │ • newsletter │                    │Foundation of │
                 │ • publicity  │                    │Co-operating  │
                 │ • appointments│                   │Patients' Societies│
                 │ • complaints │                    └──────────────┘
                 │•reports/referrals│                ┌──────────────┐
                 │ • social     │                    │Working group │
                 └──────────────┘                    │'improving Noord'│
                                                     └──────────────┘
                                                     ┌──────────────┐
                                                     │   Health     │
                                                     │information and│
                                                     │  education   │
                                                     └──────────────┘
                                                     ┌──────────────┐
                                                     │Patients' groups│
                                                     └──────────────┘
```

lower down than the level of the river into which they were supposed to be discharged, and therefore could not perform their function. To complete the picture, schools, medical centres, and green spaces for recreational purposes were ignored during the planning phase.'

The people living in the district, exasperated by these problems won a court case involving the local authority and the builders, but the compensation which they obtained provided only the most basic needs. The local priest, university students, manual workers and housewives set up the Proletarian Culture Centre. Together with 'Sotto l'argine' (Under the Riverbank) Association, it co-ordinated the demands of the people living in public housing. Different political positions were brought together in the interests of all those living in the district. Practical steps which they took included:
- setting up a purchasing co-operative, to influence the prices of local retailers;
- after-school classes, giving free lessons to the most disadvantaged young people;
- opening a district library, supplied by donations from individuals;
- producing a local community magazine.

Alliances were forged with similar initiatives in other districts of Rome, and the programmes are still carried out on a voluntary basis. A link has been made with a Christian Youth Movement, KOVIVE, which has provided the Centre with both financial and cultural contributions. Thanks to this link some young people from the public housing blocks spend holiday time during the summer in a Swiss hostel.

## Givers and receivers

A point that differentiates the perspective of local action from that of most national charities and voluntary organisations is the relationship between 'givers' and 'receivers'. Traditional volunteer-organising bodies - and much government policy - tend to see these as different people. The present view shows that the closer one gets to the inner dynamics of local action, the more this difference blurs. Yet often the people at the centre of the process feel themselves overstretched, and yearning for more volunteers to share the central responsibility.

The people at the heart of local action groups are often very **few in number** at any one time. 'The active core which keeps the groups going is less than 20 people... for over half the groups it's between five and ten people' (N,132). 'All our research on local organisations and their members points to the disparity between the small number of active members (approximately 2% of all members) who are willing and able to run groups, and who take it in turns to perform management and administrative functions, often in

*81*

**Working together: local residents in Oliveira do Douro (Portugal) meet to consider the results of the study of their locality.**

more than one group, and the large number of other members - approximately 20,000 for all the groups studied' (P,78).

In some cases there is a simple dividing line between the **activists** and the **users**, but more commonly the distinction is softened by a 'buffer zone' of regular volunteers: 'On average between eight and 35 people were actively involved in the operation... The number of more passive users varied upto 1000. It was often found that a relatively small number of "passive" users went with a relatively large number of "activists" and vice-versa ... The hard core (professionals and volunteers) who keep the organisation going are usually composed of between one and 20 workers. Five groups however reported between 20 and 50 people and four gave figures of from 50 to 100. A large hard core was mainly combined with a large number of "activists" and a greater coverage' (B,4.5).

If an organisation is to stimulate participation it is necessary that **the line between central activists, regular helpers, occasional helpers and passive users is not fixed**. People may then get drawn gradually closer to the centre. 'It is difficult in some cases to differentiate between members and users, and the terms "participants", "activists and "associates" have different connotations between one group and another... The average size of the organisations is large... but in a fair number of cases direct participation is confined to relatively few active members. On the other hand, some groups have to be classed as small even though they may have quite a wide area of influence' (S,64).

Groups in which organisers and beneficiaries overlapped a good deal tended to have a different, more participative, ethos than those where organisers saw themselves as providing a service primarily for others:

> 'A distinction can be made between *participative* groups and *service* groups. In participative groups the activists and the beneficiaries overlap to a considerable extent: being active in the group is itself one of the benefits which the group provides. In service groups there is a clearer distinction between those who provide and those who receive. Of course, there are may different balances between the extremes...At one extreme two people were running a "Furniture Bank" providing second hand furniture for those in need, which had served 8000 people, drawn from all over South East London. At the other was the Archway Project, a centre for young people and women, in which 350 local people had been actively involved in the past year, with 150 more having benefitted peripherally' (U, 165).

## Participation: concentric circles

Taking account of the different patterns of 'giving' and 'receiving', people's relationships to local groups can be thought of in terms of four concentric circles. At the centre are a small number of people deeply involved - the **core activists**. These are people who in their own time take initiative, take responsibility, who run groups and are influential in local affairs. Around them is a larger minority who are involved on a **fairly regular but less intense** basis, mainly as users, sometimes helpers but not organisers or initiators. Then there are **occasional users** and passive beneficiaries, the wide swathe of the ordinary population who benefit from amenities that have been established or protected, communications that are circulated, events that are put on, the monitoring of public services and other public effects, without having any direct contact with the organising groups. Finally there is a stratum of the people who for whatever reason are the most **isolated, immobile or socially excluded**, who cannot therefore participate in and derive benefit from the collective life of the neighbourhood.

Motivation to be active is as complex as the function of groups, and the fact that these functions are not widely understood must be one of the main reasons why more people do not come forward. An activist in a Belgian group commented: '"The problem is that most people don't want to do anything because they think they can't really change anything and have no influence on policy. In fact ordinary people are not listened to unless they form themselves into a large group" ' (B, 4.31).

However, once people have seen what is at stake they are often persistent despite difficult conditions: 'Although at other points in our conversations interviewees seemed overcome by negative feelings, questioning whether local groups could even survive... their responses revealed their commitment and devotion to their respective group, their determination to continue in the face of adversity' (P, 79).

For some of the activists the satisfaction of achievement has nothing to do with personal gain in a material sense: 'You do it for free, it takes a lot of time and you struggle with other people's problems. I don't see any advantages, I just like doing it. As long as I enjoy it and can get things done, it's nice, it's worthwhile keeping on with it. If you were always getting refusals the satisfaction would soon wear off' (N,159).

There are also unexpected personal benefits which can be a revelation to the individual: ' "You just become more open. Your knowledge has increased about the subject and about people and so on. That is very positive. Your little world has grown. You've become more aware of a lot of things" ' (N,144).

This is the inner mystery of the **key individuals** who make local action happen. These are not just volunteers - there is a qualitative difference between compliant volunteering and initiating or organising. Yet it is something that can, at least for some people, be learnt or acquired, or discovered as a potential they did not know they had. The critical moment or experience in which an activist is 'born' is unpredictable: '"My own personal involvement came when I had my little boy. We'd moved to Thamesmead three or four months before he was born and I didn't know anybody... I found it difficult to come to terms with being a mum and I read about "Meet A Mum" in a pack I was given at the hospital. It said they were a support network for people that feel isolated, lonely and depressed, and I wrote to them. They said there's nothing in Thamesmead - would I like to start my own group? I wasn't too keen on starting my own group, so I told the few friends I had about it and they said we don't want the responsibility of running anything... but I put up a leaflet at the clinic and at the bottom I said "Would anybody like to help me start a group locally?". A lady across the road said she would, and from there we actually got Thamesmead Meet A Mum going'" (U, 108).

## The excluded

A common reason why people set up groups is to alleviate the problems of deprivation. Beyond the activists, helpers and users, however, lies the 'outer circle' of people who are **unlikely to participate** in the benefits of group activity, even passively, because they are particularly isolated or excluded. 'Everything that disadvantages a person, either individually or because they are living in a disadvantaged neighbourhood, also makes it harder for him or her to participate in group activities: poor transport, lack of money, lack of safety, depressing environment, lack of facilities, being stuck at home' (U, 180). To this must be added age, illness, fear of racial or sexual harrassment, sheer lack of information on what is available, being tied down by care responsibilities. Many of these factors particularly affect women.

The most excluded people, by definition, are **difficult to observe**, but there are glimpses of them at the boundaries of group activity: 'All kinds of people come (to the Unemployed Shipyard Workers' Organisation) who are drawing benefit, and so they understand each other's situation without having to complain... Several members also know former workmates who, since the loss of their jobs, have sat at home growing increasingly lonely. An active member says "I occasionally see workmates of mine who just walk along muttering to themselves, head down. Some of them don't want to be involved, others can no longer get here..." ' (N, 171).

Relatively well-established groups were **not always receptive to participation by the most disadvantaged** people. 'It was claimed that the residents' group contained many rather vocal, better educated residents while the really underprivileged were not represented. There was a danger that certain population groups would allow their own interests to take priority at the expense of other groups' (B, 4.31). On the other hand, the Belgian researchers found, some of the more formal, professionalised voluntary organisations were better able to reach the most deprived people: 'By means of basic material and social assistance and counselling with great emphasis on a relationship of trust with those in need, the "Non-Profit Organisations" were able to reach the most underprivileged population groups which other local groups and organisations could not reach' (B,4.9).

In other cases the potential for groups to involve, or emerge from, the most needy people was depressed by the fact that authorities' approach to groups was too bureaucratic: 'Groups concerned with health and social welfare attribute their existence to the urgent need to find solutions for the underprivileged. A very worrying aspect is the magnitude of these problems and the vicious circles from which they emerge... The relationship with the administration is not always effective - quite the reverse... Attention can be given only to demand channelled through the official public services, while possibly more urgent cases go undetected, due to their failure, unaided, to formulate such a demand' (S, 68).

## Women and local groups

There are particular constraints on women's participation in local groups, such as being kept at home by care responsibilities, fear of racial or sexual harrassment, lack of money or transport, lack of confidence, training or a foothold in the world of work, and sometimes men's disapproval of their wives being active in public arenas. These factors vary in intensity from one culture to another, and are are matched by constraints in economic and political frameworks and labour market opportunities.

Whilst women's share of employment has been rising, it is clear from EC-wide analysis that women's preponderance in part-time and low paid jobs is not simply a matter of choice but a necessity in order to balance employment with family and care responsibilities (Commission of the European Communities, *Employment in Europe 1990*). The EC's **Third Equality Programme** emphasises the need to promote women's participation in decision-making at all levels.

Nevertheless women are often a **driving force in local action**, motivated by some of the very same problems. In particular, concern with the **care, health and education of children** is a unifying thread running through local action, and common to all countries, though the pattern of constraints varies considerably according to different national and local conditions. **Care for the elderly** is another area where the role of women is paramount, and where the burden is getting heavier for those involved as the proportion of carers declines in relation to the number needing care, as the elderly live longer, households become smaller, there are more single parents, more women are in the labour market and fertility declines (Fogarty, 1986). At the same time, these kinds of change in household and family composition have given **new impetus** to the formation of local action among women.

A clear underlying nexus of **women-childcare-education-health** can be detected in many of the case studies. The 'nurture' factor was a unifying force, mainly promoted by women. The whole character of local action, particularly the autonomous side of it, is evidently reliant on skills associated with looking after people in a holistic, integrated way: 'An ability to identify and empathise with people with problems or with marginalised sectors was evident... an ability to relate to the way people feel' (U,6.34).

In examining the evidence of women's involvement in local action in this research, there is a distinction to be made between how much women participate in local action in general, and the creation of groups specifically for women.

As regards formal membership of groups, women and men are often about equally visible; but in terms of taking initiative on social issues, particularly health and education, women are often the main movers. The Bannedok Patients Society (Amsterdam) was created largely by women, and the executive consists mainly of women. Initiatives in several other countries revealed a similar pattern: 'In four out of the five case study groups, women constituted the key activists' (U,6.34). 'There is a higher proportion of women than men in most groups. This is exemplified most clearly by the parents' associations' (S,65). 'The members of the parent-teacher association are almost exclusively women, who, as in the case of the cultural centre, are the ones who are most concerned with anything relating to their children' (G,165).

A **tendency for men to take the formal or high-profile positions** is common, even in some groups consisting mainly of women, as was the case in the parent-teacher association in Perama referred to above: 'It is typical, however, that of the seven members of the administrative board, four are men' (G,165). In addition to the formal unpaid positions, this trend distorts the employment pattern insofar as groups have paid posts. This was most fully analysed at Tallaght. '65% of those involved in groups were women... An analysis of the basis on which men and women were involved suggests that women tend to be over-represented among volunteers... and underrepresented in paid positions. Of 665 voluntary workers, 72% were women... In contrast, of the 210 persons who were being paid or on secondment, 27% were women' (I,99).

The constraints on women's formal participation seemed most evident in Oliveira do Douro: 'A marked feature of women's involvement in local groups is the fact that they are under-represented in management bodies. However it is women who provide essential support and do the preparatory work for events and activities... (but) their work takes place behind the scenes, invisible but essential: "Women often get a lot of pleasure out of doing things, but when they get very involved men get jealous"... Women's role is often to support men who perform management functions' (P, 79/129).

Even where cultural norms are not so strong, the domestic role inhibits as well as motivates: 'Personal circumstances can impose severe limitations on the activities in which people engage. This is particularly true of women members who, while numerically the dominant category, are usually likely to be embedded in onerous domestic and personal relationships: '"Sometimes you'd call a meeting and you'd only get a handful of parents, and you have people saying 'Where are these parents?'. The simple fact is that the parents are at home with their child and they can't get out to fight for them."' (I,114).

Indeed, the social isolation sometimes imposed by domestic work is deeply connected with how women experience the locality and come to engage with its problems: 'The Thamesmead Meet a Mum Association operates fairly informally... The nature of the organisation, run by mothers with young children, makes it hard to meet frequently. Much work is carried out over the telephone. The value that the group has for its members is inextricably related to the group's perceptions of Thamesmead's main problems. Isolation, loneliness, difficulties of transport and communication are of course problems felt by mothers with young children... "We help people make friends in an area where they would have continued to feel very lonely and isolated. It's very sad, the number of women who have said 'I used to walk around Safeways store pushing the baby buggy hoping that I'd get talking to someone'. But lots of women who said that have now got friends"' (U,6.19).

Men's attitudes and their domination of the more formal positions are no doubt contributory factors where women have set up groups specifically for themselves. 'It was important for women to gain confidence together with women. Benefits stemmed from the sharing of knowledge and in the recognition outside the home that their own experiences were valuable' (U, 6.35).

Sometimes women set up their own group as an offshoot of a general group. The residents' association which had played a crucial role in the development of Can Serra since 1973 had more men than women members, but women were now the most active, partly by means of setting up the Can Serra Women's Group in 1988 and a further offshoot, the Fiesta Committee, in 1989. 'It is the women who are most active and the major beneficiaries... There are a variety of activities which are crucially important to the personal development of the women taking part. Also a number of attempts have been made to form work co-operatives. Although these have proved unsuccessful, the experience has generally been very valuable' (S,88-9).

Several ethnic groups among our case studies had separate women's branches. Sometimes these had been initiated by the women themselves.

The committee of the Moroccan Cultural Organisation in Amsterdam Mid-North consisted of five men. Their wives were trying to get a women's group started because it was difficult for them to take an active part in public life alongside men.

In another case a similar judgement was made by community workers: 'In order to involve women in the work, it was considered essential to have a separate women's and girls' organisation with its own infrastructure. Because of the traditional values of the migrant community, separate basic operations for men and women were indispensible' (B, IV.34). Interestingly, in this locality special activities for women were seldom organised *except* for migrant women, evidently because it was recognised that the migrant community had 'separated worlds of men and women' (B, IV.42).

Whereas the role of women in local action has doubtless always been fundamental, the case studies suggest that a difficult process of change is taking place as the issue of women's role in society as a whole makes its impact in the local sphere: 'The participation of women in the residents' association has had an impact on families, bringing some of them closer together as wives gain a better understanding of their husbands and children, and dividing others, in which husbands do not accept their wives being out of the house' (S,89).

In Perama, the only group that was specifically a women's group, 'Women's House', was the oldest association in the locality. Begun in 1964 and dissolved under the dictatorship of the colonels, it reconstituted itself after the restoration of democracy. An autonomous local group run by a voluntary seven-member committee, Women's House co-operated on common issues with a variety of other local groups such as the parents' associations; it had also recently chosen to affiliate to a national women's organisation connected with the KKE (a political party). When it started, it had been a generalist group. '"The association did not talk then about equal rights and such subjects that we talk about now. There were other needs, women at that time looked at things differently. When a woman did not have a house to live in, for example, and was wondering how to set up two cement blocks and a tarred felt roof, well, the association could not go talking to her about equal rights"' (G,186). The group now focused on information for women, educational activities, the establishment of new facilities such as a nursery, and widening employment opportunities and improving working conditions for women.

Ironically, dilemmas can arise for the identity of such a group because there are also other groups which are primarily led by women, without being 'women's' groups. '"(Sometimes) women can talk with relatively greater ease, in the parent-teachers' association, whereas in the women's association ... they have adopted certain labels and have often linked their fate and their activities to a specific political party"' (G,192).

Although not much discussed explicitly by groups - nor, as will be seen, by policy-makers - **implications for the changing roles of men** also need to be worked out if women are to be able to maximise the value of their contribution to local development. The supporting role of men, whilst less common, may also be a hidden factor: 'The key women activists often had considerable home support, including the assistance of husbands or sons ... (sometimes) offering considerable support and practical assistance in terms of both resources and administration. Since there is evidence to suggest that husbands often view female activities outside the home with suspicion, this could be an important factor' (U,6.34).

There is increasing interest in the whole question of how the unpaid work of women should be recognised and treated. It has been argued that the prevailing method of economic analysis, the United Nations System of National Accounting, systematically **denies economic value to unpaid work** (Waring 1988). The European Parliament **Committee on Women's Rights** has put forward a report reflecting a growing demand for economic statistics to include unpaid work, thus giving greater visibility to women's contribution to society (Keppelhoff-Wiechert, 1991). The European Foundation has already carried out substantial work on time budget data and changing uses of working time which could contribute to this.

# Ethnic groups

Of many kinds of local grouping which could be identified for further comment, ethnic groups are particularly important for several reasons. There are both recent and longstanding ethnic minority populations in the EC, and the political exploitation of racism and anxieties about migration has grown starkly in the past few years, posing a signficant threat to democracy and human rights. Local community groups amongst ethnic minorities are an important means of assisting acclimatisation and the development of harmonious relations. Ethnicity was not pre-selected as an issue for special study in this research, and consequently not many such groups were amongst those studied in depth, but there were some important examples in Amsterdam Mid-North and Sluizeken/Muide..

Migrant and ethnic minority populations often suffer particularly from social and civic disadvantages. Studies for the Poverty Programme concluded in 1989 that there were approximately 15 million refugees, migrants, ethnic minorities and gypsies living in the member states of the EC. Over 25% suffered from unemployment and 60% of those who were employed suffered from underemployment. For refugees taken on their own (1.5m) the figures were even higher. Causes of impoverishment included:
- non-recognition of qualifications from the country of origin;
- length of the adaptation process, often from a rural to industrial economy;
- restrictive naturalisation laws and procedures;
- periods of exclusion from the labour market caused by restrictive

**Table 3.5**
**Typology of immigrant associations by orientation**

| Country of origin | Both country of origin and country of residence | Country of residence |
|---|---|---|
| Kinship and village centres | Community advice and advisory councils | Consultative institutions |
| Religious institutions | Ethnic workers' associations | Parent-teacher associations |
| Branches of home political parties | Professional and business associations | Residence or housing associations |
| Cultural associations | Sporting associations | Tenants' associations |
| Community schools eg Saturday language schools | Banking institutions | Political parties |
| Social clubs | | Trade unions |
| Homeland political organisations | | |
| Revolutionary oppositionl groups | | |

◄─────────── Trend over time ───────────►

From Zig Layton-Henry, *The Political Rights of Migrant Workers in Western Europe*. London, Sage, 1990 (with thanks).

handling of immigration, asylum and residence laws;
- employers' negative attitudes to or experiences of migrants and ethnic minorities;
- hostile attitudes based on negative images of 'aliens'.

(Bethlenfalvy, 1989).

Whilst there is a great deal of literature on migration and racism, there are few comparative studies of the local associations of migrant groups. Layton-Henry (1990) looks at such associations in Belgium, France, Germany, the UK, Netherlands, Sweden and Switzerland. He finds an abundance of migrant associations in most countries, as well as considerable variations in the political and civic rights they enjoy. Whilst all are subject to varying degrees of hostility and acceptance, the particular role of the associations shows a steady **tendency over time to facilitate integration**: 'In spite of the fact that immigrant associations are founded in order to preserve the ethnic identity and culture of their members, inevitably they play a major role assisting in the settlement of their members and encouraging active involvement in the host society' (p94). This takes the form of broadly three successive phases, from orientation to the country of origin to orientation to country of residence, each characterised by the emergence of different types of association, (see **Table 3.5**).

Information collected in this research bears this out. Both indigenous and migrant local organisations displayed a constructive approach to improving their mutual conditions and the relations between them. Affirming one's own culture and making a bridge to participation in the host society were seen as complementary not opposing aims (N,162ff; B, 4.39ff).

There are well-known difficulties in gaining the confidence of ethnic groups for 'official' surveys, and some of the **omissions** in our information are perhaps as important as the inclusions. For example, amongst groups who did not agree to provide information were all five traveller ('gypsy') groups in Can Serra (S,58). It is likely that some of the non-responding groups in the other case studies were also from ethnic minorities. This may reflect a lack of communication and confidence between such groups and the local action sector as a whole, or a mistrust of investigations bearing the hallmark of officialdom and having no researchers from ethnic minorities. The fact that many migrant groups do not have full **citizen rights** in their countries of settlement (Layton-Henry) must also be a severe impediment to the full functioning and visibility of their local organisations.

Local action is an area where an enormous contribution could be made - and is urgently necessary - to ensure harmonious relations between migrants and host communities. This could be strengthened by greater understanding of the **global context** of migration. Poverty in the countries of origin is the driving force of most migration, hence problems attributed to migration are unlikely to be solved without addressing the causes of poverty abroad. The EC's 'Lome Agreement' with Third World countries is directed towards this end. Local participative projects feature prominently in measures against external poverty and equally in measures against internal poverty, and it is likely that a great deal could be learned by making more links between the two spheres (Community Development Journal, 1991).

In the sphere of national social policy 'ethnic' issues are generally interpreted solely as internal issues; connections are rarely made with global issues, though these are taken up by government and voluntary organisations in other contexts. An enormous amount of voluntary activity within Europe is carried out to assist Third World countries in various ways and improve relations with them, and much of it is channelled specifically to **local action**

**groups** in those countries, whose concerns and methods have multifarious parallels with those of the first world (Clark, 1991). Many of the aid agencies also have local branches in the first world, both to generate donations and, increasingly, to educate the first world public on global issues. For the same reason the EC's own trade and aid programmes also support several hundred voluntary local educational projects within the member states.

EC and national government policies on trade and aid, and the policies of voluntary organisations working on issues such as ecology, third world development and human rights, frequently point out interconnections between social and economic problems on the global level and within the member states. 'Numerous developments are combining to make the world more and more of a global village. Economic decisions transcend national policy, communications and transport are making the world smaller and ecological processes such as the depletion of the ozone layer and the rising sea level pay no regard to national frontiers... Sooner or later the rich nations are also confronted with the consequences of underdevelopment, whether in the form of ecological problems, ever larger numbers of refugees or of economic instability' (Pronk, 1990).

Ethnic minorities within Europe also carry out direct personal aid programmes by sending money back to their relatives, despite their generally low pay. In many other ways ethnic minorities maintain relationships of some kind with their countries of origin, and are thus parallelling the relationships forged by Non-Governmental Organisations (NGO's) amongst the same countries, yet little connection is made by either side.

Another aspect of local action which has great importance for ethnic relations is that of culture: the exercise and communication of different cultures is a powerful way to engender respect and understanding between different ethnic and national groups. Many local cultural organisations are consciously contributing to these goals, yet aims such as these rarely appear in national cultural policies (Brinson, 1992).

Most of the locality case studies have perhaps only scratched the surface of ethnic minority experience, but taken together with background information also reviewed as part of the research, our sources indicate its great importance for the understanding of local community life, and the importance therefore of ensuring integration of ethnic aspects in strategies for local community action.

# *Chapter four*
# Local groups: how they function

This chapter goes into further detail on local community groups, focussing on how they function, both individually and in co-operation with one another and with public agencies. Key factors examined here are: autonomy, participation and the role of paid staff; funding and other resources; partnership with authorities and other agencies; and the special role of 'umbrella' bodies.

## Autonomy

In the last chapter local groups and organisations were categorised as being either **autonomous, semi-autonomous** or **externally-controlled (Table 3.1)**. To explain how groups functioned, the notion of autonomy must be looked at more closely.

The concept of autonomy as an important aspect of local action was identified in the early stages of the research, and was then built into the way that the groups in the case studies were examined. The interim report stated: 'A contemporary approach (to local regeneration) seeks to make the most of the indigenous energies within neighbourhood life. It is therefore committed to enabling people to be more self-empowering. As distict from old policies, which could be fairly simply described as controlling and providing, the approach developed in this research looks to people as directly participating in the organising of their own micro-social systems' *(Chanan and Vos, p45)*.

Autonomy was the term used to indicate this self-empowering factor. It implies freedom but adds the element of active use of that freedom to steer the course of one's life. This is not only an abstract principle but a practical necessity to make democracy work: 'That citizens should be free is an absolute pre-requisite for development, as participation in the development process is only possible where policy-makers are accountable for their actions' (Pronk, 1990).

Beyond the individual and household, it was important to examine whether citizens' groups themselves expressed and furthered the autonomy of their members and other local people. To the extent that they did so, any increase in their effectiveness and power could be taken to indicate an increase in local self-determination; to the extent that they were not autonomous but represented power from another source, they might only represent another form of dependence.

A starting point for analysis of the autonomy of community groups was a formula by Stohr (1989). He judged the autonomy of groups by four factors:
1  how the group began - whether initiated by local residents;
2  whether the resources for it were generated from within the locality;
3  whether it could make its own decisions, independent of outside constraints; and
4  whether its activities primarily benefitted local people.

Whilst these four were found to be key factors affecting local organisations, it was not found in the present research that they determined how autonomous an organisation was. An initiative might be started by local residents but be gradually taken over by external agents and lose its autonomy. Conversely, a group might acquire external resources but keep control of them, thereby increasing its autonomy. Whether an organisation benefitted local people did not seem necessarily to indicate autonomy; many externally controlled agencies might benefit local people too, and an autonomous one might also benefit external recipients (for example where its aim was to raise funds for charitable purposes elsewhere).

Whether an organisation could **make its own decisions**, control its own actions was, however, the heart of the matter. The other three aspects were important to the extent that, handled in one way or another, they increased or decreased the organisation's control over its own activities.

Analysis of case-study groups suggested that autonomous local groups tended to have certain different features from the more official types of group. Autonomous groups were **more integrative in their approach to local problems**, more adaptable and more socially cohesive. They responded to people's problems in a whole-person way and carried out social functions in a quiet, confidential way. This was less true of the more formal types of organisation.

Given the low profile of local action and the longstanding policy marginality of it - particularly of the autonomous end of the spectrum - why should it still be the case that the autonomous element is the largest? What sustains it? Where does it come from?

Surely an important clue must be the analysis of the whole area of unpaid work in the locality - mainly women's work. Traditional definitions of volunteering ignore its connections with other forms of unpaid work. For example one recent UK study defines volunteering as 'help given to others but not to family or friends' (Thomas and Finch, 1990). However, much autonomous volunteering, especially in disadvantaged areas, arises precisely from attempts to **improve the conditions and effectiveness of other unpaid work**:

> 'Over the last decade or so there has been a great increase in the number and variety of women's groups active in disadvantaged areas thoughout the country... Most are groups operating on a voluntary basis... They begin from the daily context of participants' lives... which in most cases, initially at any rate, involve a general wish to be better at what they do: at being a wife and mother, at being the manager of a family income, at being a member of a community... The needs of participants largely determine the content of the groups' activities: parenting, personal development, leadership, group development, health education, awareness of community needs, second chance education'.
> (Combat Poverty Agency, 1990, p25)

Two further elements also affected a group's degree of autonomy: first, how *participative* the organisation was - whether its members and users could take part in or influence the decision-making; secondly, to what degree, if any, it became *professionalised*: the role of any paid staff, and in particular whether they identified more with participant control or external control. These factors, already touched on in the last chapter, are looked at below in a little more detail.


# Participation

There are of course many degrees of 'participation', from merely helping out in an activity to having complete control over it. The most active types of participation are inextricably bound up with a sense of **sharing in the 'ownership' of the activity.** Local groups whose very existence and identity are under the direct control of local residents acting in a voluntary capacity are *prima facie* the groups that are most directly expressive of *some* local needs, wishes and efforts. They express the participation of their active members, but this circle may be limited. This does not necessarily mean that they are representative in a numerical sense, nor does it tell us how effective they are in achieving their aims, but it does give us concrete examples of a high degree of participation.

It is notable that **'volunteering' in such organisations has a more complex and intensive character** than volunteering in organisations which are not autonomous - which are controlled either by a public authority or by a national or regional organisation of another kind, such as a national charity, a professional non-profit organisation, mutual aid society, national religious body or political party. **Control by an outside body tends to generate a rather limited type of participation**, because its its agenda has been set elsewhere. Its model for volunteering is helping out in a prescribed role, usually under the direction of a professional, rather than under the joint

Members of the Vogelburt and IJ-Plein working group plan further neighbourhood improvements (Amsterdam Mid-North, the Netherlands).

direction of one's fellow citizens.

Clearly there are many local organisations which are not wholly controlled either by residents or external bodies but in which control is shared. We have called these '**semi-autonomous**' - a category which covers a wide range of different possible partnership structures; the common element is that there is some kind of balance between the internal and external inputs, to the extent that one could not say it was primarily one or the other.

## Professionalisation

Professionalisation, in the sense that a local organisation relies primarily on paid staff, may mean less control by local residents. However, the degree to which this is true depends on such factors as to whom the paid staff see themselves as being accountable. In some structures, organisations controlled by local residents obtain sufficient resources to employ a few staff, who are accountable to a management committee still composed mainly of local residents. Here the organisation has not lost autonomy but rather increased it by being able to mobilise greater resources to strengthen itself under resident control.

Staff in such organisations may themselves have emerged from the local resident initiative, and still share its ethos, often accepting a lower wage than they would expect to do in a 'normal' job, and perhaps in addition continuing to add voluntary time of their own beyond their paid hours. There are more than a few cases where dedicated staff with local roots have carried on in post when funding has been cut, or in order to keep an organisation going until more funding can be secured.

In other cases, paid staff are accountable to an authority or external body, or even if formally accountable to local participants, feel themselves in reality to be more accountable to an external funder on whom their salary depends. Given the clear pattern that in general higher funding is associated with externally-led organisations, staff in local action organisations are more often in this position, and professionalisation in this case tends to weight the organisation in a non-autonomous direction. There may be gains for the organisation in terms of size, ability to be systematic in method, and access to external networks and information; but there may also be losses in terms of participation, sensitivity and flexibility. In externally-led organisations this can lead to frustration on the part of local residents who feel they have little say in the running of the organisation. In semi-autonomous organisations it can lead to differences of perspective and even conflicts or power struggles between paid staff and local residents.

## Resources

Insofar as resources are meant in a material sense, they are usually taken to refer to **money, premises and equipment**. Small autonomous groups frequently make do with little or none of these, or acquire them through direct fund-raising in the locality. In some countries, as evidenced in our case studies, groups which fit a certain criterion of formality receive a modest flat rate grant (Greece and Portugal are examples). Where larger resources are given they are usually given very selectively according to formal policies of the resource-givers.

Wherever fairly large resources are allocated, they have to be accounted for in prescribed ways, and the funder or resource-giver may also require (or already have) a direct role in the management of the organisation. In other words, they are more in the nature of a contract than a grant. This kind of resourcing is based on the principle that the resource-giver knows what is needed in the locality and 'buys' it from the organisation. The conclusions chapter assesses how far this assumption is justified.

However, there is another aspect to resourcing which is fundamental yet rarely examined: **the time and effort of the local residents**. In many, probably most, groups this is the largest form of resourcing. Although it is not synonymous with autonomy, autonomous groups are heavily or even entirely reliant on it. It is also a major input into semi-autonomous groups. And even in externally-controlled groups it features as externally-directed volunteering. It is a resource which is rarely counted, and this neglect conceals the **real basis of partnership** between local residents and external bodies.

Given that the majority of groups found in the case studies were autonomous and half the remainder semi-autonomous, the clear probability is that **the bulk of resource going into local action is that of local residents** rather than of authorities or external agencies. Initiative-type volunteering predominates in autonomous groups and often has a small part to play in externally-led groups. Additionally, the kinds of groups which this research could find were obviously the more stable and formal ones. It is most unlikely that the research missed any of the externally-controlled groups because they are all of the formal kind, whereas it is likely that if any were missed they would have been of the autonomous kind, which are frequently much more informal, especially those that are small, short-term or which do not make efforts to attract attention outside their circle.

Is it not then a mere tautology to say that the more autonomous groups are less well-funded? Is it not obvious and necessary that a professionally-led group taking on a major service contract will need to be paid more than a voluntary group which is not accountable for a specific standard of delivery? Why should a largely or entirely voluntary group receive money for what it does - and does that not mean that it would cease to be voluntary?

Autonomous groups are not usually seeking to be paid for most of what they do. They are seeking *better conditions for doing it*. This sometimes involves employing one or a few paid staff to support the voluntary activity on a larger or more systematic scale.

The difference between having and not having funding for a single paid worker can sometimes mean the life or death of a group:

> 'The Home Tuition project trained unemployed people to teach English as a second language to members of migrant communities such as the Vietnamese, of whom there were a considerable number in Thamesmead. This increased the confidence, skills and employability of both tutors and pupil. Seven volunteer tutors, working with one student at a time, served 80 students a year. Despite its size and voluntary status the project was already receiving referrals from statutory agencies and requests for help from well outside the Thamesmead area. The only paid post was that of the organiser, who had initiated the project. The crucial core funding was both limited and precarious. Without it, the worker could not afford to continue, and the project faced closure at the end of 1990' (U,100).

Other key factors for which funding is needed are **premises, office costs, publicity, equipment** and, particularly crucial in areas of disadvantage,

**developmental support.** These functions can most economically be provided **through local umbrella or intermediary bodies**.

It is alarming to see that in rapid moves to 'the contract culture' which took place in the UK during the period of the research, existing umbrella bodies came to be seen by some local authorities as expendable: they were told 'We are moving over to direct contracts with voluntary groups so we no longer need you to mediate for us' - ignoring their developmental and coordinating role.

The Thamesmead investigation went furthest in discussing '**the contract culture**'. The systematising of contracts for voluntary groups (which tends to limit funding to those who can undertake to deliver a systematic service to a prescribed standard) may be only the intensification of an existing tendency for authorities to favour control and incorporation of voluntary groups rather than fostering their development.

The UK report concluded that converting government support for the voluntary sector entirely into contracts was not a policy which could succeed for long, since incorporation must destroy the voluntary nature of the groups. The policy was seen to be based on a failure to perceive that 'the voluntary sector' is made up of two quite different kinds of function: professional nonprofit service delivery, externally led and geared to contracts; and volunteer-led development which is about inner capacity building and problem-solving by residents.

## Finding the right internal-external balance

The two functions - service delivery and capacity building - are often embodied in different organisations. But they can also both be present in one organisation. Some organisations of this combined type appear to be amongst the most effective in localities. They successfully operate at the interface between voluntary action and public policy - **not losing sight of the distinction between the two types of contribution but consciously balancing them.**

The Bannedok Patients Society in Amsterdam is an example of such an organisation which was created by local residents, influenced the form of public provision and at the same time built itself an important consultative place in relation to the authorities. The Archway Project in Thamesmead is an example created from the other direction, where the authorities set up the project and the workers successfully involved local residents to the point where their influence could expand the concept and programme.

These careful and powerful 'balancing acts' cannot take place where there are *only* contracts for service delivery. They can take place where contracts for service delivery are one of two or more different types of funding. The

UK report concluded that **two different funding streams were needed, one for delivery of services and one for internal development of localities**.

For every such (relatively) successful partnership of internal and external input, many examples could be found where the potential was stifled or held back at a low level. Again, these might be from the top down or bottom up: Helping Hands, in Tallaght, was a citizen initiative with clear policy implications that could not get adequate engagement with the policy-making level - the right framework or common understanding of complementarity did not exist. The Thuishaven Centre for the Elderly, in Sluizeken/Muide, was an authority-led intiative in which the members were supposed to be able to participate but felt unable to influence events. The common element in both seems to be **a failure of the authorities to create the best conditions for the maximum input of the autonomous element** in a mixed organisation.

The same underlying tension is present in the other localities. The contract culture substitutes one aspect of a complex phenomenon for the whole phenomenon. On its own, it offers nothing in terms of helping new groups to emerge, small ones to grow larger or weak ones to become stronger; it ignores the democratic function of autonomous groups; and by tying payment to delivery of specified services it makes it harder for members to participate meaningfully in group decisions.

Failure to recognise the importance of the independence of local community action is a neglect of the roots of democracy. It is clear from the events of the last few years if not before that undemocractic societies are not only wrong in principle but suppress the internal energies which are the wellsprings of productivity, and also suppress the local corrective mechanisms which are essential to effective social policy.

## Umbrella organisations and community work

Local umbrella organisations are bodies which have a function of supporting a range of other groups in the locality. This may be an explicit aim, or a function which develops from co-operation between groups, or from the creation of new groups by established ones.

Providing help to groups is also a key function of professional community work, either directly with a selection of groups or working through a local umbrella body. The role of community work, and of the larger field into which it merges, Community Development, is critically relevant to the future of local community action, but was not a main topic of this research and can only be touched on here. Extensive literature on it is available from the relevant national organisations, some of which have been involved in the present research. The present findings imply both a need for more community work and possibly a need for considerable changes in the way community work is practised. This topic is briefly taken up in the conclusions, and will no doubt be treated more fully elsewhere. The role of local umbrella groups is of particular relevance since, to one degree or another, their functions overlap with those of community work. The present discussion should not, however, be taken to cover community work practice or community development strategy at large.

The particular concern here is to examine how far the case-study localities had organisations or services which not only helped groups on a one-to-one basis but which added cohesion to each local action sector as a whole. How necessary were they to the functioning of the local action sector and its individual groups?

**Organisations or services with a remit to provide support to local groups on a comprehensive basis are rare.** Their absence is both a symptom and a cause of the general invisibility of the local action sector. Only one of our case study localities, Thamesmead, had an umbrella group, 'Trust Thamesmead', set up to support *all* local groups; even then it did not carry out all the possible functions of an umbrella organisation but concentrated on securing funding for its member organisations and the setting up of new groups. In this respect it was highly successful, not least because it was controlled by its member organisations, not by the authorities, and could therefore be single-minded in its pursuit of their interests. A separate body, Thamesmead Advisory Forum, was run by the authorities as a means of consultation with the local voluntary sector.

A need for support and development was manifest in all the localities studied, and every locality had one or more groups which either formally or informally - more often the latter - came to be carrying out an 'umbrella' function for a limited number of other groups. The fundamental need was clear from a wide variety of evidence, not least the way in which **organisations of a certain type and size tended 'organically' to begin to take on some of these functions.** However, in the absence of a specific strategy and remit, the ability of such bodies to carry out this function for all or a majority of groups was distinctly curtailed.

Functions carried out by umbrella, or proto-umbrella, groups varied greatly from place to place. They included **providing information, building up confidence, providing space for meetings, providing a central focus for the local voluntary sector, furnishing contacts with other groups, channelling funding from external sources to groups, fostering communication across the sector such as by running a community newspaper, and sometimes representing the local action sector to the authorities.**

Umbrella-type support was of obvious importance, particularly to autonomous groups, and particularly at stages of growth and transition such as starting up, getting and accounting for grants, employing a first worker, acquiring the use of premises or facing a crisis. The condition of the autonomous local action sector was considerably affected by how far these functions were available.

In Amsterdam Mid-North, umbrella functions were more associated with national than with local organisations. The umbrellas had a sectional or 'pillarised' character which linked the group with others of its kind, and often with others of its denomination or ideological background, but not with groups of other kinds in the same locality:

> 'The pattern of a national umbrella and local branches or groups applies in many fields. For example there are three road safety organisations... which operate nationally, both separately and jointly. All three have local branches... There are also organisations which bring together members of some category of the population. Even in these cases we find the pattern of local branches and an umbrella organisation at national level. For example there are over 1800 branches of national societies for the elderly... The three national societies - a Catholic, a Protestant and a general one - also work jointly within the Central Consultative Body for Societies for the Elderly. The national societies represent the interests of the elderly and protect their rights. Local branches organise leisure and socio-cultural activities... and mutual assistance by such means as telephone circles, sick visiting, and helping with odd jobs... (but) by no means all local groups have links with national bodies' (N,222).

Local support functions were also present in the Dutch case study to some extent, carried out by the local community development service funded by the local authority. However, only 23 of the 92 responding groups in Amsterdam Mid-North had regular contact with the support service (N,133). Nationally, there were about 1000 community workers, and a survey of their work in 1990 showed that they were concentrating on a limited number of specific organisations and projects on priority topics (N,233). A similar pattern in Belgium and the UK suggests that **professional community work practice generally concentrates on a small number of local organisations with particular needs** rather than creating an overall umbrella function for the local action sector. (These were the three countries in the survey where community work was relatively well-established as a profession.)

In the Belgian case-study report, some policy-makers saw the pillarised structure of the voluntary sector as a major obstacle to integrated development at the local level. A Ministry of Culture spokesperson pointed out that subsidies to local cultural, youth and training groups had so far been carried out solely through national structures. His Ministry was trying to decentralise in order to reach the local level more effectively:

'The current subsidies to national structures have led to a compartmentalised situation at local level too. If a lecture on the environment is organised by a particular organisation, for instance, you know that it will have a particular slant... Much of the money allotted to national structures is used to maintain those structures. They gradually turn into a kind of annex to the civil service ...Instead of paying the subsidies to national, ideologically coloured structures, they should be allocated in such a way that they reach the staff on the ground. This will allow a pluralist supply to emerge at the local level, to which everyone can turn' (B,5.5).

Umbrella functions can be part of the general role of national voluntary organisations, but it is hard to identify how far national organisations in general provided practical assistance to local branches or affiliates. In the UK, which has many hundreds of national voluntary organisations, local branches were often seen as supports to the centre as much as, or more than, being supported by it. Where national organisations did provide sustained support to local branches, they often also controlled them to a large extent. At the same time, **local organisations trying to band together to create national support networks** would often have difficulty in reaching beyond a limited plateau:

'Such organisations, which have grown "from the bottom up" but are not limited to a local perspective, face enormous difficulties in reaching more than a fraction of their potential constituency... National staffing and administrative resources are often hardly any bigger than those of a local project; they may exist for a long time without reaching the critical mass that would enable them to convert the national need which they articulate into an effective national movement or service - indeed this may never happen'(U, 3.18-19).

Local organisations which officially carried out local umbrella functions were usually semi-autonomous in terms of our categories. In Oliveira do Douro, for example, there was no umbrella body as such. The nearest thing to it was the Parish Council itself, which was supported by volunteers and was close to local community action. The landscape apart from this consisted of groups falling fairly clearly into two types:

'If we cross-reference the type of activities or services of group with the voluntary or non-voluntary basis on which they are run, a recognisable pattern emerges. Whereas all the sports, cultural and leisure groups are run by volunteers (or 'devotees'), those that provide services have an operational structure that depends essentially on paid workers. A similar pattern emerges if

*105*

we look at power structures, at whether groups have the power to make their own decisions and act on their own initiative. All the sports, cultural and leisure groups have complete autonomy. (P,75).

In Perama, the Cultural Centre, founded by the municipality in 1977, had become something of an umbrella organisation by expanding its activities and its outreach functions during the past four years. From training in the realm of culture (music, dancing, theatre) it proceeded to vocational training in general - women's studies, gymnastics, computing, cutting, tailoring and shipwrighting. The last was particularly for unemployed young people and also formed part of the EC's Poverty Programme in the locality. Beyond this the Cultural Centre had grown to take on a **general facilitating role in the locality**. It took initiatives and mobilised external funding for cultural activities at large, negotiating with the municipality, central government agencies and others. It collaborated with parent teacher associations, with the Women's House and with environmental improvement associations. It also made space available for such groups. Outreach became a priority aim, partly because of the topography. The Director said:

> "'Perama is on a slope, where the houses climb up like young goats. In the northern part, that is the area that lies outside the town plan... there are no centres, no squares, no halls and it is very difficult, especially in winter, for children to go down to the three Centres, which are all situated in a line along Perama's main road. We have decentralised all our activities to the schools, which are very much nearer to the neighbourhoods, in collaboration with the parent-teacher associations... Perama is an isolated area, especially in the evening...with very difficult acess to the centre of Athens... a cultural life is essential, from primary entertainment to artistic creation... in a place which is introverted because of its conditions, its geographical location and the economic disadvantages of its residents... The shipbuilding and repair yards are one of the biggest foreign currency earners yet the government does nothing to provide facilities... in other places they have swimming pools, stadiums, recreation grounds and even skating rinks, while here we don't even have a place to put our library or a place where we can put on a comedy play for our children'" (G, 137-8).

Management of the Perama Cultural Centre was largely controlled by the municipality. Six full time workers worked alongside a number of voluntary working committees. 'Even though it is an official municipal institution, it is surrounded and supported by a nucleus of people who at the same time see it as an integrated form of initiative agency, a fact which also explains the voluntary nature of their action' (G,148). All activities were free, as is normal with municipal services in Greece. However, the Director believed there could be a lot more active participation if the structure was more democratic, and that a small charge for some activities would increase the independence and stability of the Centre.

In Can Serra, umbrella functions could be traced by the way in which **groups generated further groups in a historical chain**. A general parish group was formed in 1971. In 1974-5 it built a church which would also serve to facilitate local groups. Called 'The House of Reconciliation', this also became henceforth the name of the group. 'From the very start, its facilities were aimed at creating social, group activities. The realisation of the physical building, a collective undertaking, making no charge and accessible to all, represented "in symbolic terms, an internal structure standing for the communal spirit of the neighbourhood"' (S,69).

Most of the groups which emerged from this initiative had since become independent but it still provided the premises for most neighbourhood meetings, since there was little else available. One of the first groups to emerge, the residents' association, in 1974, became in turn a moving force in the locality: 'Its first activity was to support the battle for local rights. The residents' first successes were the suspension of (uncontrolled) building and the revision of the town plan. From then until 1978 there was a constant succession of campaigns, which created the neighbourhood's outstanding reputation' (S,71).

More recently, however, although it had spawned several further groups, the association appeared to have lost much of its momentum. Amongst a

**Supplementing state services: a religious group provides extra children's classes in the evening, Can Serra (Spain).**

variety of reasons, neglect or animosity from the municipality had played a part: 'All the signs indicate that the municipal council bears a good deal of responsibility for what has happened. By repeated snubs, such as forgetting or refusing to allow committee members to take part in the inauguration of facilities won through its pressure... the council has marginalised and demoralised the association... Party political and personal considerations have had something to do with this' (S,92).

In Tallaght, one of the key umbrella functions, **free or cheap meeting space for a range of groups**, was provided by the Dominican Priory in the older and more central part of the locality, Tallaght Village. This independent resource was evidently a major background factor in the concentration at the centre of groups which could also reach to more outlying parts. Some 40 groups in all were benefitting from the generosity of the Priory (I, 115). There were also several Community Centres in the wider locality, provided by the County Council, which housed a further selection of groups, but these two sources still left many groups with no regular access to premises. Levels of networking amongst groups were high, and a number of '**mini'- umbrella functions** seemed to have crystallised through co-operation amongst groups: '24 groups had provided resources of one sort or another to other local groups in Tallaght in the previous year. Eight had facilitated upto five groups, seven between six and 15, and nine more than 16... sharing premises, information and other resources' (I,100). Nevertheless, the lack of a dedicated umbrella group left the sector weaker than it should have been: 'The high level of activity on the ground has not as yet generated an umbrella organisation - such as exists in some other localities - to provide a forum for communication and co-operation between local groups... Inadequate premises, lack of security of tenure, general underfunding, reliance on a small number of people, lack of paid staff and limited access to information undermine the provision and development of services and activities on the part of local groups' (I,99-114).

It is clear that umbrella group functions, and community development support as a whole, are fundamental considerations in any strategy to strengthen the life of localities. These factors will be taken up again in the final chapter.

# *Chapter five*
# Making policies for local action

The relevance of local citizen action to public policies is of course many-sided; so, equally, is the impact of public policies on local action. The innate complexity of the relationship is multiplied by the different administrative and political systems of the individual countries. It is beyond the scope of this study to provide a comparative framework for all these systems. Each of the national reports contains a good deal more information on its own locality and the national context. Some comparative work has been done by the International Union of Local Authorities, but since many of the local authority systems are currently in a state of flux, it is unlikely that there is any single authoritative source which is fully up to date.

In such a volatile situation, generalising is hazardous. Nevertheless, many common underlying tendencies and tensions appear through the byzantine complexity of the different systems. There is, at least partially, a common language and climate which make it possible to discuss certain themes of universal significance without having to unravel the specific systems which operate them.

This investigation was informed by a selection of key policy themes. These relate the foci of local groups and the preoccupations of local people to the responsibilities of the public institutions and other agencies influencing policy; meanwhile the concerns and attitudes of policy-makers were investigated by a range of interviews with officials, elected members and others whose work related at different levels to the case-study localities. The relevant themes revolve around three key questions:
1  How does local action relate to the policies of public authorities and other resource providers?
2  How do policy-makers conceive and value local action? and,
3  How is local action helped or hindered by public policies?

## Common themes and national variations

The national reports themselves alert us to the great differences in context: 'This study has to a large degree been formulated in relation to the institutions and traditions of countries with well developed social welfare and social policy institutions... and with an intense contemporary debate about developing the role of the "citizens' society" and independent voluntary agencies ... In the Greek context many of these issues arise in a different form, or are arising for the first time' (G,200/203).

Indeed, each locality proved to be in something of a special situation for one reason or another, and yet the areas of common concern and even common experience were more substantial than might have been expected considering national differences.

Common themes which emerge from the views of policy-makers include:
- a general attitude of **approval** for greater citizen involvement, especially in disadvantaged areas;
- a certain **remoteness** of many policy-makers **from the autonomous** side of local action and unawareness of its extent and nature;
- much more **familiarity with the officially-led or externally-led** local organisations;
- in practice, a **preference** for supporting authority-led initiatives rather than fostering independent initiatives;
- in some policy areas an **unawareness of the relevance** of local action;
- amongst the 'social partners' (principally business and trade unions) a limited number of **initiatives** showing potential for greater involvement.

There are some striking individual national characteristics which will help us to maintain an awareness of the very different backgrounds from which we are extracting these themes:

**Belgium - Sluizeken and Muide**
Great importance is attached to 'integrated programmes' at local level but this is mainly seen as a matter of co-ordinating the work of professionals from various agencies and charitable bodies. Community development support is available to a selection of groups corresponding to social policy priorities but the model of local action is inherently dependent on professionals. There is no generally acknowledged or visible role for citizen-led groups.

**Greece - Perama**
A low level of public service provision leaves a major role for citizen action, which is vigorous in this locality but with little policy framework or public resources to support it. Some significant support does come from the (small-scale) municipality, though with a tendency to monopolise the action, and from the presence of an EC 'Poverty 3' project.

**Ireland - Tallaght**
A weak local authority system and limited social services leave a major gap in which the vital role of local groups is acknowledged by most policy-makers and residents alike. However, the varied and vigorous local action scene is held back from more coherent and sustainable development by the remoteness of the policy arena and lack of proactive strategy and key facilities to support it.

### Netherlands - Amsterdam Mid-North

The Netherlands probably has the most comprehensive support system for local action in Europe, but this still has problems in securing involvement from disadvantaged citizens; rather, it brings to the surface a 'consultation elite' of local residents. Exceptionally well developed social services - though now under strain and some contraction - make participation by citizens a complex undertaking. Nevertheless, a wide variety of groups flourish and are integrated into the texture of national life.

### Portugal - Oliveira do Douro

An upsurge of citizen action at the time of the ending of dictatorship was not sustained. A fairly static landscape of mainly longstanding groups appears to reflect a compartmentalised view of their role alongside a fairly poor level of public services. Autonomous cultural and recreational groups are a mainstay of local life, but citizen action in relation to social policy issues is largely limited to an auxiliary service role.

### Spain - Can Serra

The role of local action is largely associated with social and political reconstruction after the dictatorship. Following high-profile achievements by citizen action around stark needs in the seventies, there is a sense of uncertainty as to how to refashion itself to a situation of improved local conditions and less obvious but equally pervasive problems.

### United Kingdom - Thamesmead

A varied local action landscape continually fluctuates according to the ingenuity of numerous small initiatives in pulling together fragments of support from changing policy programmes. Alongside extensive but faltering public services, there is a mismatch between public rhetoric, which puts a high value on local citizen action, and actual policies, which increasingly neglect citizen action in favour of professionalised voluntary organisations.

If a single linking theme had to be picked out from this simplified scan, it would surely be the general tendency of policy-makers, whilst liberally invoking citizen involvement and initiative, in practice to hold on to the reins of control, sometimes to pursue important short-term interventions designed to galvanise local development, but rarely to develop **genuinely enabling long-term strategies** to foster independent citizen initiative and involvement through group or collective action.

In the absence of such strategy, the higher degree of accountability and formality which is everywhere attached to any significant level of funding **does not necessarily lead to greater effectiveness in terms of mobilising citizen energies** but rather to more professionalisation of the receiving group. Before examining more closely this crucial question of funding and control, let us review a little more fully the range of views expressed by policy-makers in relation to the case-study localities.

## Groups and policies - connections and disconnections

What groups existed, the names they gave themselves and the tasks they took upon themselves, were influenced by both internal and external factors; internally by the driving force of local needs, and by the creativity and dedication of individuals and friends. Many groups had been started by one, two or a handful of people who had both vision, personal involvement in a problem and a long-term view of the needs of the locality. Many of these people took the initiative purely as local residents in a voluntary capacity; others sometimes as professsionals working closely with local communities, though they might have to step outside their specified occupational role in order to do it.

Important external factors were *legitimation* and *support*. Both of these were at best limited and spasmodic except in Amsterdam Mid-North and to some extent in Thamesmead. Apart from the sheer *availability* of support and recognition, the way in which they were provided had profound effects on the emergence and growth of groups. Where an authority legitimates a certain kind of group and provides even sparse resources, **the ability of people in the community to crystallise action around that issue is very much improved**; conversely the absence of any public policy recognition for groups of a certain kind, or the inaccessibility of the relevant authorities, is a severe inhibition.

Equally important, the way in which the authorities define and deal with their issues, and in particular the **criteria** they attach to funding or support for community groups, have a far-reaching effect on whether groups can connect with them. Far too often the criteria are narrow and rigid, and act almost as a barrier rather than a stimulus to local involvement. This is because the general approach of local groups, whatever their 'headline' issue, is basically 'horizontal', relating flexibly to whatever concerns their members and users have, whilst the approach of institutions is vertical, guarding departmental boundaries and expertise, and constrained by further layers of bureaucracy above them.

All local groups that deal with problems at ground level see inseparable connections between, for example, health, housing, environment and employment. They may seek to deal particularly with one of these but they invariably find themselves doing so with a close attention to the others, and their efforts may convince them that they need to shift the focus. While official bodies and funding contracts tend to impose rules which make it difficult to move across to other kinds of problem, people's groups follow the 'internal contours' of problems. This has two benefits: they can easily move to adjacent problems if they need to; and they tend to provide **a general benefit in terms of social cohesion**, even where it is not part of their overt purpose.

Although we all experience this interconnectedness in our own lives, it

'Don't run down the shipyards', says the banner above the daily congestion in Perama (Greece), reflecting inhabitants' worries about privatisation. Shipyard work is still a mainstay - but only for men - whilst poor transport to other parts of Greater Athens limits other job opportunities for women.

appears to be impossible for people to do so when they are acting on behalf of large institutions. Whether they could in theory do so if institutions were designed quite differently is of less immediate importance than how to modify the behaviour of the institutions we have got. A clear lesson of this study is that, whatever may be necessary in terms of changing institutional practices themselves, local action organisations excel in providing the 'meshing' of institutional responsibilities with the intrinsic integratedness of people's lives *so long as they are given the scope to fulfil their own nature rather than that of the authorities.*

Part of what is going wrong in localities is that there are a lot of actors but **no clear map of their respective and different roles**. The idea of partnership is used to create a 'family' atmosphere, to generate the feeling that all are sharing the enterprise on an equal basis, but this glosses over the particular elements and the fact that they are **necessarily** of different types.

This may lead to competition and conflict where there could be accommodation. There may also be other potential partners who are dormant and need activating. The role of all the partners is necessary but in order for it to be managed well and become dynamic, the partners need to understand their respective special contributions, and make space for the others instead of striving for control.

Funders should recognise that the issue they wish to support will be best addressed together with a range of other activity; the boundaries should not be tied too tightly. The value of the local action as distinct from the functions that can be best carried out by the authority itself is precisely **to make the connections between issues at ground level**. That flexibility should be part of the agreement, instead of groups having to manoevre different pieces of funding in order to create the space to act flexibly. It should always be remembered that official funding is funding only part of the programme and does not thereby acquire control over the whole work of the group.

Authorities and other funders together should develop a proper culture of pluralist funding whereby instead of leaving it to the local groups to pull together packages from several sources - a tightrope act which many autonomous groups cannot or do not wish to perform - they pool at least a proportion of their funding through an appropriate mechanism which can distribute it to suitable groups without unnecessary strings.

## Policy-makers' views

Beneath the inevitable diversity in the views of policy-makers, too extensive to be summarised here, there is **an underlying tension between control and facilitation**. The ambivalence emerges as a paradox: our case studies cover countries with very different levels of provision in terms of social and local authority services. On the whole the countries with more developed social service provision (Netherlands, Belgium and the UK) were also the ones which had more fully developed voluntary sectors and a relatively extensive tradition of community development practice. This led us to an expectation that the case studies in these countries would reveal a wider variety of community groups and a more recognised role for them as part of the fabric of local democracy and social provision. This did not turn out to be true in any clear sense.

Policy-makers in Ireland and Spain often displayed a clearer recognition of the vital importance of local citizen initiatives, and at local level this was also true to some extent in Perama and Oliveira do Douro. Whilst *support* for such initiatives was sorely inadequate, in practice their *role* was often better accepted, perhaps because there were more obvious gaps in official public services: 'The comparatively high levels of involvement in local action and the high estimation of the contribution of such action to improving the quality of life in the locality... is echoed without exception in the perceptions of policy-makers... The unique role which locally-based groups and organisations can play in identifying local needs and targeting official responses is widely acknowledged' (I,128). However, the **absence of adequate decentralisation of state functions to the local level** meant that these sentiments had too few channels to be turned into reality. Autonomous groups, in particular, had little chance of making significant contact with the authorities, though some progress had been observed recently in Tallaght.

In Perama and Oliveira do Douro there was an extensive *de facto* reliance on local groups for certain purposes though the further away one got from the local level, the less acknowledgement there was of this reality, and consequently they were chronically **neglected as an aspect of national policy**. Again, the absence of decentralisation meant that there were few footholds in public authorities by means of which local groups could be legitimated and strengthened: 'Decentralisation of decision-making and programmes in a way which would lend some significance to local intervention by the "citizens' society", and the classical issue of social participation by citizens, have disappeared as subjects of political and ideological dispute... The development of forms of community action... encounters a lack of interest and an ignorance of the relevant experience and problem identification. Some of the policy-makers... identified this clear lacuna in current policy. To the majority, however, the subject either caused evident perplexity or came up against the narrow confines of administrative responsibilities' (G,248).

In Amsterdam Mid-North there was a widespread understanding of the importance of local groups together with policies which supported them; even here there were considerable problems in that groups tended to be monopolised by a relatively privileged stratum of the local population. Meanwhile, Sluizeken/Muide and Thamesmead had major problems concerning the exercise of control by authorities over groups. In Sluizeken/Muide, local groups (called 'private initiatives') were marginalised in policy even while policy-makers spoke of 'involving the inhabitants'; and in Thamesmead a national trend towards 'contract culture' sought to turn community groups into agents of official policy.

The UK development seemed to be following a United States model, where contracting out of local authority services to 'nonprofit agencies' expanded dramatically from virtually nil in 1960 to 50% of federal spending on social services in 1980 (Smith, 1990). 'The new funding arrangement means increased government intrusion into the affairs of nonprofit agencies... While contracts may allow an agency to expand services... (they) bring administrative and accountability demands that may conflict with an agency's mission... As government increasingly penetrates the nonprofit sector it undermines the civic virtues of nonprofit organisations, such as citizen participation in service development, voluntarism and community definitions of support for the needy' (Lipsky and Smith, 1989-90).

The Belgian situation is worth looking at more closely because it illustrates how even substantial decentralisation and major efforts to address local problems encounter fundamental obstacles if the element of autonomous citizen participation is absent.

Central government policy (at the Flemish Community level) emphasised decentralisaton and integration of issues. 'There are few policy areas which ought not to be involved with... tackling poverty. Action is required in the field of health policy, job creation and vocational training, education, socio-cultural development, housing and public transport. Coordinated action in different areas of authority, with poverty policy running horizontally across the vertical departmental structures, is a clear necessity' (B,5.3).

This determined vision only went so far as co-ordination amongst **agencies**. It did not appear to extend to co-ordination with local groups. At the point of delivery the 'client' was still seen as an individual whose problems had to be interpreted by professionals: 'Regulated areas of work must systematically widen their approach by seeking to achieve multifunctionality, so that they may be better able to respond to the totality of the problem of the underprivileged. In concrete terms this means that welfare workers must be prepared to refer their clients in a more active and supervised manner' (B, 5.3).

There seemed to be little recognition that **social issues at ground level are naturally linked by collective participatory organisations**; and no suspicion that the dearth of citizen-led groups in Belgium might be a major impediment to developing the integrated practice which was so ardently being sought.

Policy makers at some levels did acknowledge a role for 'private' organisations (ie local participatory groups led by one or two professional workers - the so-called 'pioneers'), but the role of such groups was mainly seen as auxiliary to the agencies. Whilst the City Council of Ghent had initiated various projects at neighbourhood level with an emphasis on cooperation and consultaton with existing groups, there was an insistence on the primacy of control over facilitation: '"The function of (local) policy at this stage is to develop and test its own initiatives using the scarce resources which we are allocated, and not simply to act as the financier of local (private) initiatives' (B,5.9). There was a tendency to see 'consultation with neighbourhoods' as merely an experimental stage on the way to a more global policy for the official agencies, not as being the beginning of recognition for a concealed sector with a permanent existence of its own.

A similar preference for control over facilitation was evident in the City's policies on helping migrants: 'Certain private initiatives have found they can play an important referral role ... Others feel that cooperation protocols ought to have been agreed with private initiatives. However, given the temporary character of the projects, and the need for structural action, it was clearly necessary for the city to take this task upon itself... As no policy plan had yet been sketched out, private interests would also have interfered with the discussion to too great an extent'" (B,5.10).

The common ground between countries and localities as diverse as those in this study is that authorities have great difficulty in facilitating local action as an independent field. If they are resourcing it relatively well they also feel they should control it or requisition it.

Thinking amongst policy-makers about local groups is rather more related to their potential usefulness to the authorities **in the narrow sense of helping to deliver programmes**, than their fundamental usefulness in terms of **invigorating democracy, reducing dependency and encouraging self-driven development**. This is not necessarily a problem that can be solved by small adjustments in policy. It points to more fundamental impediments: a general absence of the sense of people being self-determining; a feebleness in the sense of authorities and agencies being accountable to their users; a questionable degree of political and professional will to empower disadvantaged people.

These attitudes suggest that public agencies may feel that too much autonomy in local groups may be a threat to their own authority. This would be a misunderstanding of the nature of such groups. It is worth returning to De Toqueville for another clue to the relation between suffrage and interest groups:

> 'In a country with universal suffrage... associations know, and everyone knows, that they do not represent the majority. The very fact of their existence proves this, for if they did represent the majority, they themselves would change the law instead of demanding reforms... The citizens who form the minority associate in the first place to show their numbers and to lessen the moral authority of the majority, and secondly, by stimulating competition, to discover the arguments most likely to

> make an impression on the majority... Thereby the moral strength of the government they attack is greatly increased.'
>
> (De Tocqueville, Vol 1, p238)

This dictum is still borne out by present-day experience. One would only want to add that the argument is multiplied where there is not one but many minority interests - where, in effect, the majority consists of many minorities. In all the case studies there was no evidence that community groups were seeking to overthrow the authorities. On the contrary, their attempts to influence the authorities tended to enhance the legitimacy of those authorities. Most groups were wary of *any* party political affiliation, even where they had emerged through recent political liberation, as in Can Serra, Oliveira do Douro and Perama. In countries where the local authorities were weak and poorly resourced, as seen in Ireland and Greece, groups specifically wanted local authorities to have a greater role in order to more effectively deliver the policies and services they were advocating. There is not a specific, limited amount of power in a locality, which if held by one body must be at the expense of another. Power in the sense of energy and development is increased overall by a dynamic local polity, and reduced overall by a static, repressive polity.

Is it realistic, however, to expect enlightened support for *independent* local action from public authorities who also have responsibility to deliver specific programmes of social services? Are they not bound to try to assimilate local groups into their instruments? Perhaps it would be better if support for local groups could come through a different channel?

There seem to be strong grounds for ensuring that support to local action should not be completely reliant on local authorities, although they are bound to have a key role. Other mechanisms may be needed to balance the inevitable instrumental tendency. These might take the form of some kind of **constitutionally guaranteed role for independent groups**, and **national or EC-wide recognition for the role of local umbrella organisations**. The social partners might have a crucial part to play here in helping both to resource and to guarantee the independence of such organisations from government and local government.

## Funding and control: a basis for partnership?

A local authority which wanted to mobilise energy for dynamic improvement of local conditions could do no better than develop a proactive strategy for supporting its local community action sector. Whilst there is enormous variety in existing practice, it would be fair to say that on the whole the disposition of public authorities towards local action sectors is reactive, providing marginal support, and then at particular times enlisting the sector for high profile and usually short term projects on which the authority stamps its own identity.

The language of policy is imbued with a number of unwarranted assumptions underlying its dealings with local action: such as that people who are unpaid are inactive; that voluntary work is low-grade work; that the nature of social problems corresponds to departmental boundaries. People in authorities may prefer to forget, or perhaps do not know, that many of the best things done by local authorities, and many of the adjustments to policies and practice which make them work in practice, are the result of intervention by independent local citizen action.

During the past decade there has been a growing awareness of the need for public authorities and agencies to be more responsive to the people in their localities, but often this has been expressed only in terms of a provider-customer relationship. The user of services is seen as a consumer, having the right to complain, but not as a partner, having the right to initiate and to be involved in decisions. For most people there is no direct, individual route to involvement in public affairs. A vehicle is needed, and this is provided by local groups and organisations.

Most funding and resourcing of local groups is discretionary. This alone ensures that it is regarded as less fundamental than official services. Resources for it have to take a back seat whenever statutory services are under pressure - which is nearly always. The extent and nature of support for local community action is therefore very variable and depends on

**From autonomy to partnership: Radio Hospitalet, based in Can Serra (Spain) began as a voluntary and illegal venture but is now run by the municipality.**

policy-makers not only being well disposed towards it but understanding its fundamental importance.

A higher degree of funding is nearly always accompanied by a higher degree of control. This is seen as a natural consequence of the fact that authorities are accountable for their use of public money. How do they use this control? Is the amount of control exercised proportional to the amount of resources put in? Should it be? Does greater control give the funders greater 'returns' for the money? From the groups' point of view, is it worth groups going for higher funding if in doing so they lose autonomy?

Funding, whatever its scale, is only a small part of the resources that go into local action. The amount of control connected with it is often disproportionate, as if it was paying in full for a job to be done. The voluntary work that goes into local groups is not counted as part of the collateral. There is a need to develop means of measuring all the inputs on a common basis.

Groups often operate at the interface between paid and unpaid work. Grants from authorities rarely pay for more than a small proportion of the total economic input into the work of a participative group. The nature of the partnership is masked by the value attached to the cash input as opposed to the unpaid labour input. If a value were imputed to the unpaid labour this would make visible the real basis of the partnership.

In most local groups **the main 'funder' is the local residents**, particularly the core activists. It might be argued therefore that in any partnership they should have a proportional voice in determining the direction of the group. It is more appropriate for the authority to see itself in a supporting rather than controlling role.

There are examples, and these are very important for the future of this area, where a dynamic accommodation can take place between the 'top down' and 'bottom up' inputs. The examples which have been examined suggest that success is dependent on the fact that both sides understand that they are **representing different resource bases**.

Authorities which fund local action tend to frame their requirements in terms of service provision and categorical issues. This may be effective insofar as they succeed in turning those groups into satellites of the public services, but to treat them this way does not make the most of their inner nature. It is a misconception to suppose that citizen action groups are good at performing standardised functions or mobilising surplus, inactive voluntary labour. They mobilise people's capacity to solve problems or address difficulties jointly, which has a quite different dynamic. One of their greatest strengths is their flexibility, but this is difficult to reconcile with standardised methods.

Some of the commonest misconceptions of citizen action that can be found amongst authorities in many countries are summarised in **Table 5.1.**

**Table 5.1.**
**Local community action: shifting the paradigm**

**Conception**
1 The unpaid population is basically inactive and dependent on services.
2 Local community action is good at mobilising voluntary labour, thus ...
3 ... providing supplementary services cheaply.
4 Local action groups are mini-versions of national voluntary organisations.
5 Authorities and charitable bodies are the largest funders of local action.
6 Authorities are the main source of the long-term view of local interests.
7 Local action is more effective if it is closely directed by policy.
8 Authorities should therefore direct the action.

**Correction**
1 The unpaid population is highly active doing unpaid work.
2 Local community action is good at organising people's problem-solving energies, thus...
3 ... reducing their dependence on services.
4 Local action groups have a quite different perpective from national 'voluntary' organisations, which are highly professionalised at the centre.
5 People's unpaid work constitutes the largest funding of local action.
6 Long term local groups have a longer-term view of local interests than authorities do.
7 Local action is more effective if it has a strong autonomous element.
8 Authorities should therefore support and facilitate the action.

To generate powerful local action, with accommodation between residents and authorities, would require a much clearer view of the characteristic strengths and weaknesses of the various 'players'. All players need to understand each other's characteristic and appropriate roles, hence what each is bringing and where it fits in. This process should clarify the different and complementary roles in partnership and create more proportionate influence among the partners. It is inadequate to regard a sector of dozens of groups, involving between a third and a half of the local population, and addressing a wide variety of key social issues, as a marginal player.

A summary of the characteristic strengths and weaknesses of six key partners in local action is set out in **Table 5.2**. The simplifications could be disputed but it is some such 'map' as this which is required to guide the way to a proactive strategy for local action, discussed below.

*121*

## Table 5.2.
## Six partners to local action

|  | 1<br>Independent citizen action | 2<br>Large local authorities & public agencies | 3<br>Small municipalities |
|---|---|---|---|
| **Strengths** | • Direct expression of citizens' needs<br>• Flexibility<br>• Whole-person approach<br>• Close to informal networks<br>• Mobilise dynamic volunteering<br>• Long-term view of interests of the locality<br>• Non-cash economy | • Major resources<br>• Key responsibilities and powers<br>• Democratic legitimacy<br>• Expertise<br>• Economies of scale | • Close to local action<br>• Democratic legitimacy<br>• Some resources |
| **Weaknesses** | • Few material resources<br>• Non-systematic methods and services<br>• Lack of access to policy<br>• Limited scale of individual groups | • Poor inter-agency co-ordination<br>• Rigid issue boundaries<br>• Paternalistic view of people with disadvantages<br>• Short-term view of interests of the locality (political fashions)<br>• Tendency to requisition rather than facilitate citizen action | • Tendency to monopolise local action<br>• Dis-economies of scale |

| 4<br>**National or specialist voluntary or charitable organisations** | 5<br>**Social partners (business, trade unions and others)** | 6<br>**Professionals working in the local community** |
|---|---|---|
| • Channel extra resources into deprived areas<br>• National networks and information<br>• Expertise<br>• Mobilise auxiliary volunteering<br>• Independent of government | • Major resources and potential<br>• Examples of successful involvement<br>• Independent of government<br>• Key role in training and labour markets | • Skilled in facilitating citizen action<br>• Understanding of impacts of policy at local level<br>• Values-basis for empowerment of people with disadvantages |
| • Paternalistic view of people with disadvantages<br>• Centralised perspective obscures nature of local action | • Generally under-developed in this sphere<br>• Unfamiliar with dynamics of local action<br>• Paternalistic view of people with disadvantages<br>• Priorities may conflict with local interests | • Insecure employment basis<br>• Difficulty of developing strategy |

# Chapter six
# Conclusions and recommendations

## Introduction

Each of the seven national studies on which the present report is based came to conclusions and made recommendations about the role of local community action in its own country. To a lesser extent they also drew implications for the EC as a whole. Whilst there are of course considerable variations from one country to another, there is also a remarkable basic underlying unity to these conclusions. There are few recommendations peculiar to one country which are not also relevant to other countries. Undoubtedly, in developing better national and local frameworks each country would do it somewhat differently, taking account of national traditions, priorities and states of development. Even so in the end there are more areas of common or complementary experience than might have been expected from national and cultural differences.

In reviewing the conclusions of the different national studies there is no intention to imply that the combined findings necessarily apply in each country. That is for analysis and consideration separately in each national context.

This concluding section has five parts:
- firstly a completion of these introductory remarks and a discussion to **locate the study in the framework of EC policies**;
- then a **review of the national conclusions**, highlighting aspects which reveal particular consensus or interesting contrasts;
- thirdly a presentation of further **conclusions which emerge from the overview** presented in this report;
- fourthly a proposed outline of **strategies** for local action, and
- finally, **recommendations** of the report.

The recommendations cover a range of action from things that local groups themselves might do, through local and national government, to the EC. Each level of action is to some extent dependent on facilitation or legitimation at another level. Whilst there is a great deal of talk about 'partnerships', it is rarely clear just who the partners are and what are their specific contributions. Recommendations that are specific to particular levels will only work if complementary action is taken at the other levels, and all levels need to **share a vision** of the way local community action could work best.

If there is a central principle that could lead to more effective local community action it is a threefold link between 1. **EC social and economic policy**; 2. **national and regional frameworks for local government**; and 3. **local government frameworks for local community action**. This research opens the way to tackle the question of what subdsidiarity means when it is followed through to the level of the locality: how is it to be applied not only as between the EC and national governments, and not only between national and local government, but also between local government and the local community action sector? If the various partners could adopt a common understanding of their complementary roles, a **powerful local development momentum** could be released. Reviewing the evidence from the seven countries and a variety of other studies one gets an impression of deep currents of local energy looking for the right outlets and all too often not finding them.

## The role of the European Community

The European Commission has long recognised that the advent of the Single Market, making the Community economically more powerful, also has uneven and adverse effects within some of its parts. The increasing concern with social policy also inherits long-standing social concerns at national level. The EC recognises a necessity to compensate for the unequal economic 'starting positions' of its member states, particularly following the accession of Greece, Spain and Portugal. One of the major planks of EC development has been the concept of **spatially uneven distribution of advantage and disadvantage**, and measures at various levels to overcome this: macro measures like the **Structural Funds** and micro measures like the **Social Action Programmes** and a variety of research, information and exchange networks.

Spatial unevenness of development occurs not only between countries and regions but also in cities, towns, villages and neighbourhoods; **macro measures targeted at regional level need to be further targeted to more detailed levels** in order to be sure of reaching the concentrations of disadvantage even within a statistically disadvantaged region.

Innovative programmes directed at local areas have pointed to the need to achieve active citizen involvement if they are to work well. 'From these policies, the elements of a common philosophy are emerging, which has to do in part with the areas of action which should be emphasised but is more particularly concerned with methods... Neighbourhood revitalisation schemes could use a common method which can be summed up in two words: **project** and **partnership**... Insofar as the action programmes centre on specific areas, they cannot be carried out without building up partnerships and mobilisation among the associations of inhabitants in the districts and housing estates concerned' (Commission of the European Communities, *Building the Future*, 1990, p8).

The '**project culture**' also picks up on a wide variety of national initiatives such as the programme of the *Delegation Interministerielle a la Ville*, which has organised partnerships for improvement in 148 of the most highly stressed neighbourhoods in France, seeing them as a 'laboratory for rehabilitation'.

However, the now substantial tradition of local projects, both national and European, has not yet yielded a clear exposition of how the 'citizen participation' element really works, or what prevents it from working. This is a **debilitating gap in strategy**.

Comparing our picture of local community action sectors with reports from the various innovative local programmes, it is possible to identify to some extent where the gaps lie, and what some of the key difficulties are in **concretising the principle of citizen involvement**. One common feature is the submergence of the participation element within 'local integration' initiatives which are highly geared to institutions rather than citizen groups. An example from the Transnational Team on Migrants and Refugees is characteristic in this respect:

> 'Systematic and synergetic action with the following agents at local level have been developed:
> - municipal authorities
> - churches, parishes
> - union branches
> - vocational and professional training centres
> - private entrepreneurs
> - chambers of trade
> - public social and health service
> - manpower and employment initiatives
> - banking and investment corporations
> - job placement agencies
> - self-help groups
> - political parties
> - local newspapers
> - schools and educational authorities'
> 
> (Bethlenfalvy, 1989)

Whilst local people in their own right are nominated in just one form, self-help groups, the endeavour as a whole is about the bringing together of *institutions*. All of these institutions, unlike community groups, have a readily recognisable status, and professional resources, to bring to such a partnership. To achieve this kind of forum around problems of local development may have a potential for powerful integrated actions by those bodies, but has major drawbacks as a vehicle for the participation of local residents. It must be well-nigh impossible in such a forum for local residents to have a meaningful voice. There is firstly the numerical disproportion implied in the listing, and secondly no attention to the *different nature* of the resident base.

Another way in which the potential of participation may be masked is by concentration on the process of intervention rather than on the situation to be changed. The intervention ethos and tradition is supply-centred rather than results-centred. A report of the *Neighbourhoods in Crisis* network, studying local authority-led initiatives in a variety of disadvantaged urban areas in Europe, expresses the need for citizen involvement in intense terms: 'The common feature of these policies is that they emphasise a comprehensive action dependent on a partnership coordinated on a precise territory with the purpose of involving the local inhabitants in the development process... It is in effect the professionals and the community representatives who carry the programmes... In all the towns visited the same ambition drives on the action of the steering committees, that is **to make the inhabitants the real agents in urban development**. Is this simply a worn out phrase or is it a reality?... The whole art lies in giving inhabitants access to the public decision-making places' (Jacquier, 1990, p55).

This still leaves local residents' **own organisations** invisible. The existence of such organisations is perhaps implied in the role of 'community representatives', but nothing is seen of the sphere of independent local community action. The focus is still on the forum created by the institutions, where presumably participation is to take place, and not on discovering the network of residents' own groups and organisations where, our studies display, participation *does* take place. This centralising tendency is surely part of the cause of the inertia identified in some of the cases studied: 'All the institutions are represented, but precisely because the joint action is carried out strictly on the basis of representation, it reunites, without possibility of modification, the static sum of the situation already in existence' (Ibid, p42).

The present research suggests that local initiatives would develop greater momentum by first **mapping out the local community action sector**, on a wide territorial basis, and then by examining its pre-existing dynamics and limitations, assessing where strengths can be built upon 'indigenous' social territory rather than just in the institutional forums created by the initiatives themselves. 'An alternative way to resource local action may be to start with an issue and examine the manner in which it is being addressed by the actions of various groups and organisations and consider how the different unique contributions may be strengthened' (I, 161).

Such a mapping should be comprehensive as to the types of local organisations sought, not pre-judging the relevance of groups by their size, informality or overt purpose. The present findings show that **participation, social cohesion and support are spread through recreational, religious, sporting and social groupings as well as those explicitly devoted to self-help or social policy issues**, and that some of the smallest groups are also some of the most intensive in the support functions they provide for their members.

For professionals in such initiatives to appreciate the importance of this process, it may be necessary to overcome lingering assumptions about the passivity of 'inactive' people. Local community action is largely hidden from view in all countries, which has perhaps allowed apparent differences to become exaggerated: 'The participative dynamic, the self-help and the community movements characteristic of the British tradition contrast with more of a consumer type of attitude which is often the characteristic of continental societies' (Jacquier, p 18). This generalisation, disproved by the present study, is more of a tribute to the hidden nature of local action than to substantial national differences.

At the level of partnership in plans for the improvement of a locality, citizen participation should not be assumed to mean participation by individual representatives in forums dominated by institutions; it could mean the creation of a structure which **balances** a forum of **all the relevant institutions** with a forum of **all the relevant citizen groups**.

One of the most productive measures that the EC could take in this area would be a programme to develop a common culture of support for local community action by all appropriate authorities and initiatives, based on best practice. Most EC innovative local programmes are focussed on labour market measures. They inevitably leave the nature of the local community action sector itself, its permanent role in social cohesion, in the shadows, because it acts mainly in the area of 'economic inactivity'. This sector, the present study shows, is generated not mainly by attempts to improve income, though it includes some of these, but by attempts **to meet needs in the equally fundamental area of *unpaid* work**. Poverty of course takes many forms, some of which require solutions outside the framework of the labour market, or which are pre-requisites for improvements in labour market participation, such as better amenities and conditions to support carers of children and other people.

By clarifying the real dynamics and dilemmas of local action the options for the role of the EC will become clearer. If there is to be something that might be called a European approach to local community action it will emerge from many different directions. The EC has a major role to play in facilitating common understandings, frameworks, exchanges of experiences, and in how it uses its resources to influence the deployment of greater resources of other kinds, not the least being the great hidden resource of people's unpaid work in localities. However, a more penetrating concept of local community action should inform not only the action programmes but the management of the Structural Funds, and the deliberations of both the Economic and Social Committee and the new Council of the Regions set up following the Maastricht summit.

# Review of national conclusions

## The need for local action - and a government framework

All the national reports agree on the importance of local community action and the need to make it more effective. Its condition, and the obstacles which face it, vary from one country to another, though with a wide overlap of common factors. All the reports see a need for enabling policies at national as well as local level:

> 'A central objective of policies at the various levels, local, regional, national and EC, should be to increase the power of local action' (P,38)

> 'The objective of building up independent local capacity should be given a central place in social policy. Government should re-examine its aims towards the voluntary sector and reassess the impact of current policies on the capacity of local voluntary sectors' (U,185).

> 'Innovations in this sector require co-ordination and co-operation with national policy agencies and corresponding adjustments to legislation and policy' (G,310).

In none of the countries except possibly the Netherlands did the researchers find an adequate national framework already existing, despite apparent consensus on the need for it:

> '(There is) the absence of any single body in the state sector whose responsibility is development of policy regarding local action... As a starting point there is a need to clarify the relationship between the state and the operation and objectives of local action' (I,162).

> 'The role of local action is to create a problem-solving and support framework to make the lives of the underprivileged bearable and to argue on this basis for structural intervention by the authorities to achieve actual solutions... There is widespread agreement as to the need for an integrated approach to deprivation, for co-ordination at government level and for co-operation/consultation at local level, but in practice these working principles appear still to be in their infancy and to be facing all kind of obstacles' (B,8.1.2).

> 'Local action... merits a department at the highest political level. This could be a subdirectorate-general of the Ministry of Social Affairs or, at a more local level, of the governments of the Autonomous Communities. The need to maintain a census of local groups, to channel their activities, to promote contact with other institutions and to formulate strategic policies ... point to the practicality of setting up a department to act as co-ordinator' (S, 146).

## Cautions

Along with this call for a national framework for local action go certain cautions about such a framework taking the wrong form or being based on the wrong premises. There are warnings against illusory policies which do not really tackle the issue:

> 'The role of local action can only be given its full value if it is embedded in an external context which creates the structural conditions not only for combatting the adverse effects of social and economic changes but for avoiding them... We must be on our guard against unrealistic expectations. Government initiatives in the area of local action are limited to the welfare sector despite repeated calls to other government sectors for genuine co-ordination with the aim of constructing an integrated approach' (B, 8.3).

> 'Associated with the strengthening of local action in Portugal is the need to increase ... state policies to correct ... imbalances in the area of social policy ... to strengthen social rights, which are at present manifestly inadequate. (We must) reduce the risk of making rights and benefits dependent on voluntary, non-public initiatives' (P, 8.38).

## Decentralisation and local authorities

It is clear from the equally explicit calls for decentralisation that the national framework should be *an enabling* one, applying the principle of subsidiarity towards regional and local bodies, rather than *directing* and controlling all the action from the centre:

> 'The most important policy measure (in the state sector)...is the introduction of legislation to provide substantial decentralisation (for) the implementation of

> programmes at local level... The primary pre-requisite for the development of local action, the utilisation of local potential and the mobilisation of individuals for the purpose of coping with problems, is the existence of planning and decision-making procedures targeted at local level' (G, 298).

However, these measures must be distinguished from illusory decentralisation:

> 'Decentralisation does not just mean having local branches of the administrative authorities and at the same time maintaining a bureaucratic, hierarchical structure but the development of a system of local programmes for implementing general policy' (G, 298).

The Irish researchers describe the need to 'reduce the distance between local action and policy-makers':

> 'This distance includes geographical, institutional, organisational aspects and factors arising at the interpersonal level... For local groups and organisations the consequences vary from minor misunderstandings to sheer absence of information and inability to establish working relationships with public sector agencies. For policy-makers this situation can substantially reduce or skew their understanding of local action and reduce their capacity to develop policies sensitive to local groups and organisations' (I, 166).

The Dutch report advocates what it calls 'administration close by', a practice which some commentators there claim already exists but which in the light of this research is seen to be only beginning: 'Nearness ...is not primarily concerned with shortening the walking distance to the meeting rooms of the district council. It is concerned with the manner of administration which offers the urban dweller good service and couples access to the political process with receptiveness to the influence of the residents' (N, 274).

## The local government framework

In the same way as the national framework must be enabling rather than controlling, the local authority framework must apply the same subsidiarity principle in relation to the local community action sector:

> 'There is an urgent need for clarity regarding the role of public and [voluntary] initiatives in local action. The present trend for channelling subsidies for local action to the municipal authorities and municipal schemes has

> given rise to a great deal of resentment on the part of private initiatives... no concrete indications have been given concerning the manner in which private initiatives should fit into the new policy approach. Properly worked out co-operation between public and private bodies is a *sine-qua-non* for an efficient and integrated approach to local problems' (B, 8.4).

Ironically, in the absence of a comprehensive national framework, the problem with the role of public authorities is not their monolithic nature but their fragmentariness:

> 'Currently the tendency is to think about and resource local action in terms of individual groups and organisations. This is related to and reinforces the current structures of funding. These tend to emphasise a one-to-one linkage between the source of funding and the specific local group and the issue it addresses' (I, 161).

The official perspective which interprets the work of local groups solely in terms of their lead issue masks the complexity and variety of their function. This results in **a polarisation of perspectives between funders**, who believe they are engendering innovative local action and who tend to be only interested in the parts of it which they have funded, **and practitioners** on local projects, who invariably feel they are trying to do something more complex and more long-term than any one of their funders understands. In order to do it they have to continually rearrange bits of funding and support from a number of agencies, each of which is under the illusion that it owns or has created the action. A disproportionate amount of time has to be spent on this as funding is almost always short-term and each funding source tends to keep changing its criteria. The amount of information and ingenuity required puts this byzantine world out of the reach of many local groups.

## Towards co-ordinated local strategy

Clarifying the local government role means that **local authorities need to have a strategic overview of their whole local community action sector**. Remarkably, this seems to be lacking almost everywhere. Local authorities tend either to treat the local action sector as remote and marginal, or to recognise only a limited circle of organisations which fit its formal criteria, or which are carrying out contracts directly supplementary to the functions of the local authority itself.

The whole culture of local action, including EC initiatives, is carried out on the basis of individual projects. The position in Spain is stated starkly but is in essence not exceptional:

> 'Spain lacks a policy for guiding local action... Most of the groups and associations are in a chaotic state. In essence, funding is organised through institutional contacts, usually on a personal basis...communication with the authorities necessitates maintaining contact with various individuals who work at different levels and deal with different issues.... The authorities should set up bodies to support local action, to assess the benefits derived from such action and to monitor activities, management and administration. It could also serve as a channel for dialogue between the authorities and local groups or asssociations' (S,132/146).

Having an overview of the local community action sector is an indispensible part of maintaining an overview of the locality itself:

> 'The locality is under pressure. Systematic attention should be paid to how events in Banne-Buiksloot develop, if any further slippage of the locality is to be reported before it is too late. A neighbourhood network which would send out such signals would offer some help in this respect' (N,274).

It is only with a comprehensive overview that all the local elements can be brought into play:

> 'Programmes for local development can dramatically increase their effectiveness by recognising the significance... of the whole spectrum of local action, from the more informal campaigns by local residents and the networks of friends, family and neighbours to the more established organisations' (G,310).

A co-ordinated view of the sector would be equally necessary to engage many external agents whose present contributions are either haphazard or non-existent:

> 'A great many potentially important agents play scarcely any part in community development. All the "instruments" present at local level should be used... Societies, employers' organisations, the health services, the so called "hard" sectors and the new social movements are all important partners' (B,31).

In order to foster the local action sector, local authorities themselves need to be suitably empowered by central authorities where this is not the case:

> 'Policy in all sectors will have to strengthen the role of local authority participation in decision-making and

> planning and in the substantial decentralisation of state programmes' (G,303).

> 'The devolution of decision-making power to the local level would facilitate the role of local action in improving the quality of life... There is a clear need for active consideration of the relationship between local groups and organisations and any reformed system of local government' (I,167).

## Dangers of incorporation

Recommendations for a strategic approach by local authorities do not mean that authorities should *try to direct* the local action sector. Support should mean support for independent growth, not the incorporation of the local action sector into the authorities themselves:

> 'In order to offer people meaningful participation a local organisation needs to determine its own affairs. This reinforces the need for the "arm's-length" approach to funding. This does not mean supporting organisations indiscriminately but publishing criteria of support and then supporting unconditionally those organisations which meet the criteria' (U,187).

The **contracting out of services** from local authorities to independent local organisations might be a desirable development 'imparting a fresh stimulus to local groups and leading to huge financial savings' (S,147), but **should not be confused with stimulus of the local action sector's independent role**. Contracting out of services has to be clearly distinguished from fostering local community action, which is more fundamental, more long term, and involves basic principles of democracy:

> 'This should be a quite different mechanism from contract culture, where the bidding organisation has to deliver a service pre-determined by the controlling agency' (U, 187).

A distinction needs to be made between taking responsibility for ensuring that the locality has a flourishing independent local action sector and, on the other hand, seeking to institutionalise and professionalise this sector:

> 'The introduction of mechanisms to accredit local action seems worthy of consideration (but) exclusive use of the formal system of education and training could lead to the displacement of many of those currently involved, who would be replaced by more highly educated actors; this

*135*

would result in the institutionalisation of an invaluable and irreplaceable bridge between actual lived experience of local problems and the administrative system whose purpose is to solve them' (P,41).

Instead there should be

'flexible systems of training and accreditation... forming part of a plurality of models... respecting and affirming cultural diversity' (P,41).

Incorporation of local action into the authorities' own programmes would in fact destroy it: it can only complement the work of authorities by being independent of them, as the Irish report explains lucidly:

'A distinctive feature of local action is the unique space that it occupies. Here we emphasise three aspects. First, local action tends to occupy an intermediate position with respect to the private domain of family and personal networks and the public domain of statutory provision. Second, local groups and organisations adopt a considerably broader perspective than do the statutory services regarding the relationship between the experience of a problem and the services and activities relevant to its alleviation. There is no simple one-to-one correspondence between a specific problem and the types of services provided to address this. Third... the activities of local groups and organisations provide a unique basis for rendering transparent the linkages between the personal problems of people and public issues...Local action is engaged not solely in the delivery of welfare goods but in a process of empowerment and enfranchisement of local people... Its unique role vis a vis statutory provision is not as an alternative or potential replacement but as complementary to such provision and to public policy more generally' (I,162).

The problem of reconciling the need for local authority strategy with the need to avoid local authority dominance suggests that there must also be some other basis for safeguarding the independence of local action. National governments need to find a way **to require and resource local authorities' fostering of local action and at the same time to guarantee the independence of local action.**

This tension between support and incorporation also has implications for the role of 'umbrella' bodies and development agents, whose crucial role emerged so clearly in the case studies. It is affirmed in the conclusions in terms which illustrate the different national bases on which this role could be built or enhanced:

'It will be necessary to give particular emphasis to the development of relatively independent centres at the level of the municipality itself (for small municipalities) and at neighbourhood level, which provide support, premises and equipment... There are few such centres in Greek cities... The creation of such centres would seem to be the best immediate way of covering, with relatively modern means and considerable economies of scale, some of the terrible deficiencies that local agencies are experiencing, and of doing so in a way which provides the best focus for local community life... They should be managed by experienced professionals who have close links with the local community, and there should be active and equal participation by the network of natural leaders and active citizens' (G, 305-6).

'Co-ordination of the various initiatives will become increasingly important. Local groups should be encouraged to set up networks by neighbourhood or by interest. This would justify the provision of resources to fund the appointment of professionals with special coordination skills. Support should be given to all aspects of life rooted in local action - local newspapers, movements, campaigns, festivals etc' (P,42).

'Local intermediary or umbrella groups and community development projects... are usually professionally staffed organisations with a specific function of co-ordinating, supporting or developing local voluntary and community group capacity. These crucial functions are not widely understood and need to be reassessed and strengthened' (U, 189).

These issues are taken up in the general conclusions section which follows.

# General conclusions

Beyond those reached at national level, several further conclusions suggest themselves as a result of the overview of local action. This part of the discussion falls into five sections:

i   Fundamentals
ii  Relationship with the voluntary sector
iii Relationship with poverty and disadvantage
iv  Women and unpaid work
v   Strategies for developing local action

## Fundamentals

The present research shows that important functions of the local action sector include:

- as a source of personal social networks;
- as a means of organising mutual aid or mutual activity;
- as a supplement to the provision of social services;
- as a monitor and corrective to social policy;
- as a means of defence of common interests, for example against the despoilation of the local environment;
- as an alternative, free-access citizen power base, countervailing corporate or institutional power.

The local community action sector is important in all localities, but it is likely to take a different shape according to the prevalence of particular problems or preferences in each place. For example what particular countries want or need most from their local action sector will differ according to whether people see themselves as aiming to *build up* or to *modify* the public welfare services in their country.

The fact that the local action sector is fundamentally voluntary, although it may include a number of paid staff, means that public authorities cannot create it. But strategies to recognise and support it can make a great difference to whether it is strong and effective. Local groups are a natural, endemic phenomenon. There is a strong argument for saying that democratic societies should have an obligation to **provide a certain level of background support to enable local community action sectors to flourish**. The basis for local action must exist everywhere because freedom of association is a *sine qua non* of democracy.

It is essential that the support of authorities should be based on '**arm's-length**' principles; that is to say, indirect support guided by advice, not direct control. If this sector is controlled by the state, that undermines its voluntary nature. Attempts to co-opt it into the state would suppress or destroy it.

## Relationship with the voluntary sector

The local community action sector cannot simply be identified with the voluntary sector. There are rules under which 'the voluntary sector' in each country operates, but local groups that have the necessary formal constitution may be only the tip of the iceberg of local action. To clarify some of the key differences:
- while each country has specific rules or traditions for its voluntary sector, **many local organisations exist outside the rules**, yet are often performing the same functions as those within the rules;
- where the criteria are rigid, the **emergence or recognition of new groups**

is prevented or discouraged;
- **national voluntary organisations have a different perspective** and policy agenda, and are different types of organisation, from local groups, even where those groups are members of the national bodies;
- some local community action may be **led by authorities**;
- a huge range of informal local community action takes place **outside groups**.

National voluntary organisations have a major but not determining role to play in local action. The largest part of their work at local level is concerned with two functions: firstly mobilising voluntary labour to perform certain social services; secondly contracting to deliver certain services on behalf of public authorities. Important as these functions are, they are only a part of the local action mixture, and it may be argued they are often fairly marginal to internally generated problem-solving activity which lies at the heart of this sector.

Nevertheless national voluntary organisations also perform important functions at local level, and indeed **could do much more if they adopted appropriate policies**. They may provide opportunities to link with specialist networks which go far beyond the locality; they may provide help with funding and resources; and perhaps potentially most important of all, they may provide a third partner between local citizens and local authorities, providing extra legitimation, experience and information.

A minority of local groups are members of national voluntary organisations. It may be argued that even unofficial local groups exist broadly under the umbrella of the national voluntary sector; that their legitimacy is generally understood by analogy with constituted groups, and their interests are promoted at national level by the major voluntary organisations. This argument is put into acute question by our findings. National voluntary organisations behave quite differently and have a different perspective. Whereas the national voluntary sector is often highly professionalised and understands 'economy' to mean primarily charity fundraising, local community organisations are genuinely voluntary and are more concerned with the *unpaid economy* that is closely connected with the daily life of the household and the neighbourhood, care for children and elderly, and the improvement of local amenities. All this unpaid work is a huge part of the total national economy, but usually uncounted and unanalysed. In an overall economic analysis, this part of the social economy is much larger than the national voluntary organisations.

The dominant agenda of national voluntary organisations is to do with issues like charity fundraising, the provision of supplementary social services and the professional management of volunteering. The primary concern of independent local groups is *how to get people together to solve a local problem, meet social needs or influence authorities*. Their concern is therefore with social policies in the broadest sense and with local development and democracy. Whereas the professional charities are usually **specialising in some form of public service**, local groups are often **dealing in microcosm with complex interactions between public services, private households and local communities**. Thus paradoxically, they have a much broader perspective than many national charities. They also generate a much more complex and initiative-taking type of volunteering. This breadth and depth may be hidden from the gaze of policy-makers by the way in which the national organisations are taken to represent the whole voluntary organisations sector.

These differences are not clarified, as yet, by the introduction in 1990 of a specific department of the European Commission services (DG XXIII) to deal with the 'Economie Sociale'. It is not clear how far in practice the definition of this sector incorporates local associations as well as co-operatives, charities and mutual aid societies. The initial agenda of the service appears to be oriented much more to the concerns of national voluntary bodies. It is important that local action groups should be given greater recognition. The importance of the social economy cannot be understood without a greater focus on the local level, not just on work co-operatives and other employment initiatives but on **the life-support role of the whole range of other citizen groups**. There is a vital need for the hidden social economy to be better recognised, ensuring that the local viewpoint is represented in national and international deliberations.

## Relationship with poverty and disadvantage

Examination of how people organise themselves to address problems in disadvantaged localities illuminates local self-organising as a *universal* element. An effective local action sector probably plays a major part in the quality of life and protection of local interests in many advantaged areas. This has hardly ever been researched. Equally, in other areas (especially some new towns) the absence of such a sector is likely to be a disadvantage to local people even if they are individually well off. The strategy for local development in a deprived area will be a particular variant of the fundamental principles.

This investigation has confirmed the crucial role of groups in local development and social cohesion, and an auxiliary role in solving people's personal problems. These functions could be much strengthened with better resourcing, better strategy and a better understanding of how to maximise the effectiveness of the community groups sector.

The investigation shows that, despite poor conditions, the local community action sector already plays a vital role, and could play a larger one, in improving conditions in disadvantaged localities, and in maintaining good conditions once achieved. This is different from saying that local groups can directly solve problems of poverty and exclusion. To show that such groups reach *some of* the most disadvantaged; and that such groups are an effective stepping-stone back into society for *those who get involved* in them is not to say that they reach and help all '*the disadvantaged*'.

Should anti-poverty strategy devote all its efforts to the most deprived and excluded people, leaving established groups and organisations to fend for themselves? This would seem to be self-defeating since the groups are evidently playing, at least, an important preventive role, assisting people to maintain a level of social contact and activity which is undoubtedly connected with their general ability to manage their lives, and hence not to slip into the category of the 'most deprived or excluded'. The groups themselves are often struggling to survive, are rarely reaching their full potential because of present conditions, and **their collapse could only increase the number of the socially excluded**.

Equally, local groups have a role in creating or maintaining certain benefits for the locality as a whole, which bring some general benefit even for the most deprived. The existence of a vigorous local groups sector means that agencies seeking to find ways back into society for excluded and isolated individuals, or seeking to engage the local action network for new groups specifically established in order to involve the most deprived, have a variety of footholds for these purposes.

Everything learned in this study about how groups communicate and co-operate with each other, and about the crucial role of umbrella groups, indicates that **new initiatives will have a far better chance of survival where there is a vigorous local action sector** - so long as they are able to emerge at all. The caveat is important: some societies have formalised the criteria for recognition as a local organisation in such a way that it is difficult for new groups to emerge and gain recognition. This seems to be particularly true in Portugal, but equally in the very different conditions of Belgium: although professional community work was maintaining some important groups in Sluizeken and Muide, there was little sign of encouragement for the growth of a diversity of autonomous groups. The only groups that could be found playing a significant role in relation to social policy issues were either formally established ones or those reliant on continuous community-work support.

However, conditions were also far from ideal elsewhere. It was probably easiest for new groups to gain official recognition in the Netherlands, but it seemed that a multiplicity of small groups somehow did not create an overall climate of participation. In Thamesmead there was great variety in the types of group that were functioning, but public policies and funding were so unstable that survival, let alone growth, was a continual gamble.

It is clear from the relationship between groups and informal local action that if the groups sector is to flourish it needs a certain fluidity, for new groups to emerge, try things out and become established or take another course, for older groups to diversify and sometimes to die off, as changes take place in public issues and the composition of the local population. Rigid criteria for the recognition of groups are likely to prevent development. Any

*141*

strategy for strengthening the local groups sector must include provision for **a 'ladder' of development** from the small, informal and experimental, through transitional, to the long-term and established. This may include a need for professional community-work assistance at certain stages, but if groups become permanently dependent on such assistance, the goal of greater autonomy for local residents may be lost sight of, and the community work skills not released for new groups.

Thus development in the local action sector is an essential part of an anti-poverty strategy, but it is doubtful that it can in itself form the front-line. Building up the strength of groups to take on collective issues often requires focussing on people who are not themselves in a situation of severe personal need.

Poverty isolates. Groups work best at a level above deprivation. The key movers need to be close enough to the problems to know them inside out, but also must not be overwhelmed by them. To build up these groups is therefore not usually to work with the *most* deprived and isolated, but it may be necessary at times to try to start groups specifically amongst some of the most deprived. Because involvement-oriented groups may be fairly small, there may need to be quite a number of them at any one time. If one is trapped in a private space, creating new public space may be the best way out!

A distinction must be made between *the alleviation of personal poverty* and *the alleviation of disadvantaged local conditions*. Both are necessary, and by making the distinction clearer, and challenging the way in which so much literature in this field treats these factors as interchangeable, the relationship can be better understood.

To concentrate all efforts on alleviating personal poverty while ignoring disadvantaged local conditions is futile in that the gap between personal improvement and opportunities in the surrounding environment will remain impossibly large, and the only way that individuals will be able to permanently improve their situation would be to abandon that locality, leaving behind an even more homogeneous population of the most deprived.

On the other hand, to improve local conditions in a general way, without relating this to the position of the most deprived, is likely to leave the problem of poverty untackled, even aggravating it by conncealing it behind apparent improvements. This has been an observable, and much criticised, tendency in some high profile local improvement schemes which have focussed on improving the physical conditions of the locality without addressing the conditions of the people in the locality (like London Docklands).

**A local response to poverty demands a dual strategy**: availability of personal social-work help for the most deprived and dependent, and availability of community work for groups. It also needs a better mutual understanding between these two roles, so that they can make appropriate use of each other. Community work, where it exists, is sometimes attached to social work teams, but this often leads to frustration because the community work is usually the junior partner within an overall strategy that does not distinguish clearly between the needs of individuals and the needs of groups. Groups, in the sense of local organisations, are sometimes confused with therapeutic groups run by social workers, but individuals who need intensive help are rarely (at that time) the people who can carry out the complex responsibility of leading a public initiative. There is no evidence that deprivation can be adequately tackled by groups consisting only of the *most* deprived.

In a follow-up seminar to the research in Belgium it was observed that 'In welfare projects that are expressly oriented towards the most deprived groups the attention of the community worker is almost completely absorbed in relief work ... there is little or no time for a neighbourhood-oriented approach' (Berghman, 1991, piii).

Teams of community workers or led by a community work strategy are rarer, but an innovative evaluation of such a team in Wrexham (Wales) carried out at the same time as the field research showed a powerful increase in the capacity of the whole of the local community action sector (Bell, 1992).

The dual strategy should take account of the differences found between providing services and getting people involved. Social workers wanting to make use of the groups sector need to be clear which kind of function they want to call on for a particular client. Some groups are good at converting users into participants. Turning the receiver into the giver-and-receiver, is perhaps, paradoxically, the greatest benefit that can be conferred, in that it gives the person a greater sense of reciprocity, hence of inclusion and autonomy. It is the more intensive types of group that can do this - the types of group that do not necessarily deal in large numbers of people. An anti-poverty strategy, without expecting groups to deal with primary causes, might want to stimulate and reward groups' ability to be more receptive to the underprivileged and to try and draw them more towards the centre of the action.

The community work contribution should be targeted on an **overview of the local community groups sector**, ensuring that the sector as a whole is strong, with groups of all kinds in sufficient number. This provides the context for any work helping to start new groups specifically involving the disadvantaged.

## Gender and unpaid work

Looking at local action through the experience of women puts familiar issues into a clearer perspective. Women are key players in certain aspects of local action. In many respects women and men are equally active, but men are more likely to take formal or paid positions. Women are however more often the driving force and the 'doers' on a range of issues that are fundamental to local life, especially on health, education and welfare. Their activity is all the more significant for the fact that it often springs not from leisure but from needs associated with continuous unpaid work such as the nurture of children, people with disabilities and elderly people.

Women are often in a key bridging position between the unpaid economy and the paid economy. Much 'women's' work is done in the locality - the locality is a working environment for the unpaid economy. The way women's activities flow from unpaid, neighbourhood-based work to paid work and back, both daily and in life-cycles, is a major element in social cohesion, but women who have both paid employment and care responsibilities have least free time of all population categories.

Many EC measures are rightly directed to improving women's access to the labour market. More recently this has brought, in turn, concern with improving the facilities for women who have dual responsibilities, eg creches at work, but these policies are seen as important principally because they facilitate labour fluidity. A framework is needed for considering paid and unpaid employment together, as **different sides of a single integrated economy**. In 1991 the EC Women's Committee put forward a resolution to the European Parliament to give women who work at home comparable working conditions and benefits to those in paid employment. The resolution is basically about work within the household, and rather residually about local community action, but it would be a major step forward in recognising the dual nature of the economy and beginning to bring unpaid work in general into policy debate.

For women to have better access to the labour market implies a need for changes in lifestyle amongst men as well. Men would need to take a greater share in household and caring roles, to free more of women's time for paid work. It has been argued that this would also have many other benefits for men, and for society generally. For example Mies (1986) sees connections between men's isolation from direct caring roles and their violent exploitation of women, nature and the Third World. In research such as that of Waring (1988), women's experience has led to an alternative analysis of economic growth which emphasises the fundamental value of the home, the locality and co-operative networks. From this perspective the concepts that dominate the development of the EC are very 'male', and this leads to a considerable imbalance in objectives and policies. Local community action may be seen as part of a household and community economy whose characteristics are cyclical development, reciprocity, the balancing of

'Economic inactivity' is hard work: washing clothes at a communal wash-house in Oliveira do Douro (Portugal), where some houses have no water supply.

productivity and consumption, and resistance to the violent exploitation of women and nature worldwide (Shiva, 1989).

The EC has placed a major emphasis on encouraging increased mobility of all kinds. There has been a neglect of the counterbalancing element of stability - of home, environment and locality. There is too little recognition of the positive value of stability and the disruptive effects of intensified mobility (and greatly increased transport) on family life, on psychological security, on social networks, on quality of life and environment. For a successful local community action sector, a certain degree of residential stability is essential. Public policy that rests on assumptions of strong local life needs to reconsider the impact of increased mobility.

In policy discourse there is a general unreflectiveness about the social costs of too much mobility in terms of its effects on personal and local life support systems. A degree of stability is essential to meet the needs of children, people who are elderly and people who are disabled, and indeed the needs of those who look after them; but stability is equally of importance to those who in some respects are highly mobile. The life cycle of all individuals moves from local dependency to mobility and back to dependency, and everyone attaches a positive value to an attractive, interesting, friendly, safe, historically continuous home locality.

The women's perspective relates strongly to these factors. In trying to accommodate this perspective, it cannot be overlooked that the EC itself does not yet reflect equal opportunities policy at its senior levels. The senior posts of both politicians and professionals are overwhelmingly in the hands of men, and whilst there is no predetermined relationship between gender and attitudes in any individual person, there can be little doubt that a better balance would produce a more integrated view of the relation between social policy and economic development.

# Strategies for developing local action

Every country, region and even locality has particular conditions of its own. This research has shown that there are large areas of common experience and common need, which need to be widely recognised, and around which specific variants can be built. These are the basis for the following approach to local strategy. The framework falls into two parts, the first on principles and aims, the second on methods.

## Principles and aims

The approach is based on the fresh assessment of the current condition of local citizen action which constitutes the findings of the present research.

The local community action sector exists probably everywhere to some degree except where it is specifically suppressed, and it is unconsciously relied upon by society for a whole range of low-profile but essential social functions. It achieves important effects despite a low level of public recognition and resourcing, and a lack of overall strategy; but the level of its effectiveness is often held back well below its potential. It is an area promising huge benefits but which is currently existing at the margins of policy, achieving far less than it could because it is starved of resources and understanding. It is not the panacea to all ills; it is not a substitute for public services; but it is a factor which enormously enhances both public services and private quality of life, which holds back worse crises and which could, with more proactive policy, make a greater contribution to alleviating crises which have already become manifest. Its full contribution is badly needed in a society which is going through major disturbances and readjustments and which needs above all more flexible, imaginative and effective approaches to social problems.

The approach to a strategy for local action must be based primarily on what it is that the local action sector does best and which is not done, or not adequately done, by public authorities, private households, national voluntary organisations or other institutions.

These distinctive features of local citizen action are that it:
- integrates social, economic and environmental issues;
- involves local inhabitants in an active 'ownership' role;
- takes a flexible, whole-person approach to people's problems;
- takes a long-term view of the locality - a personal 'life-investing' point of view;
- makes public services work more effectively by both critiquing and supplementing them.

The aims of most initiatives in this field are usually stated in relative terms - 'to improve', 'to ameliorate', 'to intervene'. This is a natural reflection of their origin in a problem-solving and crisis-driven ethos. Whereas this research is also orientated to problems and in particular to recent changes in social and economic conditions, especially for disadvantaged people, it indicates that coping with change is an accelerated form of coping with life. The role of citizen-led groups in a locality is often a long-term one, compared with some official initiatives, and the role of the local action *sector* is a permanent one, while individual groups change, grow and die. The viability of any particular initiative, whether originated by residents, authorities or other agencies, is bound up with the condition of the local action sector as a whole in that locality, and any given social issue will be addressed by a variety of groups, either more or less explicitly. A strategy to overcome disadvantage and strengthen independence, or equally a strategy to reform the public services by more citizen involvement, should therefore address itself to the condition of the local action sector as a whole.

This holistic approach allows us to make the leap from relative and short-term aims, which are always unavoidably vague and difficult to evaluate, to aims which, if not permanent and absolute, are at least long-term and concrete. This seems essential if intervention is to achieve lasting improvements.

The present findings may be used to construct an outline picture of **what an adequate and effective local action sector would consist of**. This will still, no doubt, be subject to different interpretations, but it is a major step forward as compared with the prevalent fragmentation of efforts in this field.

A locality with an effective local community action sector will have these characteristics:

- a wide range of independent community groups reflecting the major social issues, both explicitly and implicitly;
- one or more umbrella groups having the resources and remit to strengthen and support local citizen action as a whole;
- conditions which encourage new groups to emerge without preconditions and which enable them to grow at their own pace and under their own control;
- availability of contracts where suitable for non-profit organisations which wish to and are capable of taking on systematic responsibility for a particular service;
- availability of separate funding and support for citizen group functions which are not appropriately dealt with by contract methods;
- additional incentives and support to assist groups to reach and involve more of the most deprived people in the locality;
- full public awareness of what groups are available, what they do and how to get in touch with them;
- strong networks of co-operation amongst the groups;
- good contacts with, or presence of, a wide spread of national, regional and international voluntary organisations;
- public awareness of their right to start a new group if they wish to, and the help they can get in doing so.

## Methods

The main steps can be sumarised as:
1 **surveying**;
2 **general resourcing and partnership**; and
3 **community development**.

### 1 Surveying the local action sector
The condition of local action sectors should be studied for the whole population within whatever is the most convenient administrative boundary. To study who is reached, who isn't reached, who participates and who is

left out one needs a **demographic** basis, not an 'organic' community basis. 'Natural' communities will never entirely correspond to administrative boundaries, but to try to relate policy only to 'natural' communities would merely lead to tautology: those who are left out would evidently not be part of the assumed community.

The process developed for this research itself could provide a starting point for **building up a profile of a local action sector**. For longer-term purposes a database could be used to keep track of groups as they emerge and change. Contact with a wide range of the major national voluntary organisations could be plotted. Efforts could also be made to find out about organisations which have ceased to function, and why, or which have tried to get going but not succeeded. Assessments of local need could be compared with the profile of groups, and special initiatives taken to fill gaps.

**2 General resourcing and partnership**
In allocating resources, special value would be placed on autonomous activity by local residents, whether within wholly autonomous or semi-autonomous organisations, on the basis that a critical factor regarding the function of the group in increasing the regeneration of the locality is whether the members, users, activists, volunteers, feel that the organisation really **belongs to them**. This is not necessarily a matter of where material resources come from but of the basic constitution and ethos of the group: is it seen as a service provided or organised entirely from the outside or as one which to a significant degree belongs to and expresses the will of local people? In the latter case it is much more likely to last, to elicit active local participation and to adapt and extend to meet new problems as they arise.

This priority should not, however, mask a neglect either of the use of suitably professionalised organisations to **carry out contracts to a prescribed standard**; or of well-established and **traditional voluntary organisations** which may be carrying out some important social function in a static way. If the aim of innovative organisations is to overcome disadvantages, the aim of established organisations is to maintain improvements once attained. They remain a vital part of the landscape and may well be carrying out important preventive functions without explicit policy. **Alliances and co-operation should be encouraged between new and old organisations.**

Wider partnerships, involving both groups and authorities, and drawing in support from industry, trade unions and national voluntary organisations, should be arranged by the most suitable body, which may be the local authority or a general umbrella organisation for this sector in the locality. Chapter Five stressed the importance of maintaining a realistic appraisal of the respective interests and limitations of partners, not concealing their different interests in an assumption of commonality. The partners - particularly from the local residents' side - need to **retain a separate base in their own constituency**, and need to **retain the sense of a distinct viewpoint and negotiating position** if they are not to become a 'consultation elite', absorbed upwards into the official structures and thereby increasingly cut off from the bulk of the local population.

An awareness of these essentially different perspectives should remain even within the partnership forum:

i Independent local action has greatest freedom of action, the freedom to work laterally across problems and issues; freedom to take up positions critical of authorities or other power holders when necessary; strongest connections with informal local networks; most scope for voluntary roles with real initiative and responsibility. However this part of the sector often has low material resources, limited information, and limited access to wider networks.

ii National voluntary organisations can contribute well-tried models for local branches; networks of specialist information and contact; but may also have agendas and processes that derive more from their national role than from the needs of the locality. In some cases they may be highly professionalised, and expect to control rather than facilitate the local volunteering which they mobilise.

iii Public authorities are likely to have relatively high material resources and access to information, networks and training, but are liable to approach issues in a 'vertical', sectoral and compartmentalised fashion. They may tend to try to impose regulations and procedures that bear little relation to the needs of the locality or the natural dynamics of a local group.

## 3 Community development

Any new practice in this field stands to inherit a substantial tradition of professional Community Development (CD) practice and theory. Community Development has played an important, if uneven, role in social policy in many European countries over the past twenty-five years. In 1989 the Council of Europe adopted a resolution from the Standing Conference of Local and Regional Authorities of Europe calling for wide recognition of CD as an instrument for local and regional government, and a number of specialist national bodies and international networks are working to extend and adapt Community Development to meet current conditions (McConnell, 1991).

Much analysis of Community Development took place during the first and second phases of this research, when a wide range of literature and experience from this area was consulted (see Boucneau, Decleir et al, 1989). The fieldwork phase, which has provided the main basis for this volume, was relatively little concerned with further analysis of CD practice except insofar as it emerged as part of the support to the local community sectors under examination. It was playing a significant role in Amsterdam North and in Sluizeken and Muide, and had played some part in the development of groups in Tallaght and Thamesmead. Without more historical investigation it is difficult to say what role it may have played in the development of the local community action sectors taken as a whole.

The present study owes a great deal to the concepts and experience of community development built up over the past twenty years. However, it also throws into question whether the inherited CD approach is adequate to the contemporary challenge. Community Development offers some of the most relevant available experience on which to base a plan for how a local action sector can be supported and developed. However CD practice is often too narrow in approach and has on the whole avoided the question of demonstrating results. It also tends to focus exclusively on deprivation, leaving it unclear whether the reason why CD is needed in deprived areas is because favoured localities don't *need* local action or already *have* local action. The focus on local action as a permanent feature opens up the question of how not only to *achieve* good conditions but how to sustain them. Community Development practice, like many other forms of social innovation, has also taken place mainly through small isolated projects rather than district-wide or locality-wide strategies. An observation from German background material could be repeated in many countries: 'Regarding German practice there are a lot of local projects that comprise single elements of a possible new strategy of urban planning. They have arisen as a reaction to local problems and as a consequence of the engagement and creativity of local people… These might show the way to achieve new forms of co-ordinated acting (but so far) they are mainly single experiments' (Froessler, 1990).

Any new strategy to strengthen local community action needs to take full account of community development experience but also to add:
- clearer orientation to demonstrable results;
- sense of scale, of strengthening the whole local community action sector rather than concentrating on a few groups;
- clearer distinction of roles between community workers, community groups and communities, so as to be able to demonstrate how the community work helps the groups and how the groups help the community;
- forging alliances between groups of different kinds;
- reorientation to a wider range of public authorities and corporate bodies, to lever resources from all sectors;
- more examination of how local action works for relatively advantaged as well as deprived people, to see how gains can be consolidated.

Clearer, more comprehensive goals will make possible better forms of evaluation leading to improvements in practice and more confident policy.

# Recommendations

These are addressed to policy-makers in the European Community at various levels: in the Commission and Parliament; in the Economic and Social Committee and the new Committee of the Regions; in the member states individually; and at regional and local levels.

*151*

Since the subject matter is local life, much of the necessary action falls within the responsibilities of national, regional and local government, and within the actions of local organisations and initiatives as well as to the various bodies of the EC. Action in localities involves partnerships of the different levels and sources of authority and resources. Such partnership is seen for example in many of the initiatives supported by the Regional Development Fund, the Social Fund, innovative actions such as the Poverty Programme, and information or action research networks such as LEDA and ERGO. It is also seen in individual national and regional initiatives.

These recommendations do not aim to identify the precise role of each partner or each level. The intention is rather to propose the main elements of a common approach and a common understanding of complementary roles which should be fostered and facilitated, in the first place by the main decision-making bodies of the European Community. The recommendations fall into four key areas.

## 1 Localities, local action and social cohesion
Policy-makers in all social fields should **acknowledge the indispensible contribution of local community action to achieving and maintaining good living conditions; and gear social and economic programmes to strengthening local action and bringing it out of the shadows so that it can play its full role**.

Local community action is increasingly invoked and relied upon as a basis for social policies, but its own functioning is rarely an object of such policies or of strategic planning. This study shows that local community action is a universal factor in the internal growth and management of a locality, crystallised in a range of autonomous and semi-autonomous groups. Such groups, and the capacity of people to form new ones, are a vital part of the fabric of social cohesion, assisting people to cope with change and exercise some influence over it. But the conditions for local action are frequently difficult; in particular, funding, support and recognition for groups is generally low and insecure. Strengthening the conditions for local community action would enable other social policies to be made more effective both in cost and social terms.

Specific measures might include:
- mounting a new EC social action programme on living conditions and the role of local community action sectors in their improvement;
- creating national, regional or international community development strategies to foster local action, especially in areas of disadvantage;
- examining why some public authorities have little or no tradition of fostering local action to complement their responsibilities while others do, and instituting such practice, particularly in planning, transport and environment;
- implementation of the principle of social cohesion at local level by ensuring localities' freedom from disruption and deterioration;
- ensuring that an understanding of the place of local community action

in contemporary life and democracy is learnt in schools, and available in further and higher education.

## 2 Local development strategy
At the level of local strategy, policy-makers should **institute measures to strengthen the local community action sector, especially in localities with disadvantages, and should do so on an 'arm's-length' (non-controlling) basis, notwithstanding other policies which may be developed to contract individual non-profit organisations to deliver specific services.**

The local community action groups sector is a permanent feature of localities but its capacity at any time is deeply affected by the level of recognition, support and co-ordination on which it can draw. Policy-makers should recognise that to try to improve conditions solely by successive waves of short-term, piecemeal projects, which has been the pattern of the eighties, is inefficient. Specific measures might include:
- recognising the legitimacy and value of community groups of all types and at all levels of development, and relaxing rigid criteria of recognition and funding to encourage the emergence of new groups and the diversification of the sector;
- developing a co-ordinated view of the sector, and monitoring its condition;
- making a clear policy distinction between
  a  delivering some parts of public services through contracts with non-profit organisations, with full accountability, and
  b  building up the general capacity of local people to be more independent of state services by a variety of autonomous groups and by a stronger autonomous role in partnerships with public agencies.

The second of these policies should be evaluated at a strategic level but the individual groups should maintain their independence and their own ways of working. This may be achieved by:
- improving the resourcing of the sector particularly by better funding; by better spread of funding amongst eligible groups; by improving the access of groups to relevant policy arenas; and by creating or enhancing infrastructure such as:
  - umbrella group functions (services to other groups, strengthening networks and co-operation);
  - community work stimulus and assistance to disadvantaged groups;
  - free or cheap premises for groups;
  - training for local residents who take on group responsibilities.

Whilst the preceding measures are important firstly for all localities and secondly in particular for disadvantaged localities, within localities of all kinds there are individuals who will not easily be reached and special measures are needed to enable them to participate in local action. These might include:
- fostering of special community groups targeted amongst them and better public transport and security;
- care relief arangements;

- better access to telephones;
- confidence-building;
- more outreach from, and receptivity in, established local groups and organisations;
- ensuring that all residents have full civil and political rights;
- ensuring freedom from racist, sexist or other forms of intimidation.

### 3 Economic value of unpaid work

Policy-makers should **take steps to recognise the economic value of unpaid work and modify social and economic analysis to take account of this.**

Voluntary action of all kinds is usually unpaid; it is generally regarded as taking place within the area of 'uneconomic activity' and is not subject to economic analysis. Similarly poor local conditions are regarded as a social misfortune rather than an economic cost. But the strengths and weaknesses of the whole field of unpaid work, of which the locality is the workplace, and the assets and disadvantages of the locality itself, represent real costs and benefits to society; they also show up economically in levels of skill and enterprise, and in the degree of local people's reliance on public services. Strategic local development requires both social and economic analysis of these areas. Initial measures might include:
- ceasing to use the terms 'active' and 'inactive' in economic statistics and replacing them with 'paid' and 'unpaid';
- identifying in all economic figures the missing category of unpaid adults working in the home and community;
- in funding partnerships, recognising voluntary input as a form of funding, conferring the same rights and influence as cash funding.

### 4 Four key partners

In addition to public authorities at all levels **four other types of body are identified as key partners in local development. Each has a special role to play.** This concluding section of recommendations highlights selected areas of action to be addressed by these, complementing each other and the recommendations above.

NATIONAL VOLUNTARY ORGANISATIONS are widely assumed to represent at national level the interests of voluntary action at local level. This study shows that the majority of local groups and organisations are not members of national organisations, that they operate differently and that the experience and perspective of local action is not well reflected in the national organisations. Hence there is often no real voice for local experience in national or large scale policy-making. The national bodies should:
- consider how they can better facilitate people at local level to take local action as well as contributing to the efforts of national bodies;
- recognise that the main basis of local action is autonomous action by residents, and that externally-mobilised volunteering is supplementary;
- make it clear that they do not claim to represent the local community action sector as a whole, and consider what they can do to assist that

sector to develop its own national voice.

THE SOCIAL PARTNERS should:
- create more initiatives to mobilise input from industry and trade unions into local community action, not limited to financial support but by using their many forms of resources;
- integrate the local community perspective into their strategic planning;
- recognise local community action as expressing needs in areas of unpaid work' and examine how they can help to improve its conditions;
- consider ways in which they can help local action by secondment, premises, and encouragement to employees;
- consider that they may have a key role in establishing, resourcing and guaranteeing the independence of local umbrella groups.

LOCAL GROUPS AND ORGANISATIONS themselves should:
- become more aware of themselves as a local sector with its own viewpoint, and develop a more collective local and national voice;
- take more measures, and seek more support, to extend their activities to reach and involve the most deprived and isolated people;
- re-examine their own economics and insist on their unpaid input being counted as part of the funding of local groups so as to improve their negotiating position in relation to funding and partnerships;
- find ways to ensure that the local perspective is heard at national and international levels, and seek to develop their networks to ensure that their concerns are heard at EC level.

COMMUNITY DEVELOPMENT AND SOCIAL INTERVENTION INITIATIVES should:
- re-examine their practice and theory in the light of the results of this research, as well as social and economic changes and trends such as decentralisation and the mixed economy of welfare;
- work at more strategic levels, taking account of the whole local action sector and creating alliances between established voluntary organisations and innovative community groups;
- focus more on outcomes, distinguishing their own role from that of local groups, and distinguishing the groups from the communities at large;
- demonstrate their contribution to permanent local improvements.

# *References*

NATIONAL STUDIES

The seven national final reports of the research project are:

**Belgium:** Patricia Boucneau. *Coping with social and economic change at neighbourhood level.* Brussels, VIBOSO, 1990.

**Greece:** Dimitris Emmanuel and Effie Stroussopoulou. *Coping with social and economic change at neighbourhood level, The Greek case.* Athens, Dimitris Emmanuel Planning and Research, 1991.

**Ireland:** Carmel Duggan and Tom Ronayne. *Coping with social and economic change at neighbourhood level: final report.* Dublin: Work Research Centre, 1990.

**Netherlands:** J Foolen, A Harberink and K Vos. *Coping with social and economic change at neighbourhood level, final report.* 's-Hertogenbosch, Nederlands Instituut voor onderzoek naar Maatschappelijke Opbouw, 1990.

**Portugal:** F Rodriguez, S Stoer, P Vieira and A Monteiro. *Coping with social and economic change at neighbourhood level, Portuguese case study.* Oporto, Cooperativa de Ensino Superior de Servico Social, 1991.

**Spain:** Ricardo Suarez and Gloria Rubiol. *Coping with social and economic change at neighbourhood level.* Barcelona, Institut de Treball Social i Serveis Socials, 1991.

**UK:** K Shanks, J Bell and G Chanan, *Social change and local action in an urban area.* London: Community Development Foundation, 1991.

OTHER REFERENCES

Baine, Sean et al (1992) *Changing Europe: Challenges Facing the Voluntary and Community Sectors in the 1990s*. London: CDF/NCVO.

Barde, Jean-Philippe, and Button, Kenneth (1990). *Transport Policy and the Environment, Six Case Studies.* London, Earthscan 1990.

Bell, John (1992). *Community Development Teamwork - Measuring the Impact*. London: Community Development Foundation.

Benington, John (1989). *Poverty, Unemployment and the European Community: Lessons from Experience*. Warwick: Local Government Centre.

Berghman, Marita (1991). *Coping with Social and Economic Change at Neighbourhood Level, Seminar 3 May 91*. Brussels: VIBOSO, 1991.

Bethlenfalvy, Peter von (1989). *Results and Prospects: Refugees, Migrants, Ethnic Minorities and Gypsies in Europe*. Louvain: University of Louvain, Transnational Team on Migrants and Refugees.

Boucneau, P., Decleir, M. et al (1989). *Coping with Social and Economic Change at Neighbourhood Level, An Annotated Bibliography*. Dublin: European Foundation for the Improvement of Living and Working Conditions.

Burton, P., Forest, R., and Stewart,M. (1987). *Living Conditions in Urban Europe*. Dublin: European Foundation for the Improvement of Living and Working Conditions.

Brinson, Peter (1992). *Arts and Communities: Report of the National Inquiry into Arts and the Community*. London: Community Development Foundation.

Carley, Mark, ed. (1991). *The Social Charter and its Action Programme*. Europeran Industrial Relations Review. London: Eclipse Publications.

Chanan, Gabriel (1991). *Taken for Granted: Community Activity and the Crisis of the Voluntary Sector*. London: Community Development Foundation

Chanan, Gabriel and Vos, Koos (1990). *Social Change and Local Action*. Dublin, EFILWC.

Clark, John (1991). *Democratising Development, The Role of Voluntary Organisations*. London: Earthscan Publications.

Combat Poverty Agency (1990). *Towards a Policy for Combating Poverty Among Women*. Dublin, CPA.

Commission of the European Communities (1990). *Building the Future*. Brussels: CEC (DGV)

Commission of the European Communities (1990). *Employment in Europe 1990*. Brussels: CEC (DGV).

Community Development Foundation and National Coalition for Neighbourhoods (1991). *Taking Communities Seriously. A Policy Prospectus for Community Development and Local Democracy*. London: CDF.

Community Development Journal (1991). *Community Development in 1992, The European Dimension.* Oxford University Press: Community Development Journal 26:2, April. Other issues of the journal regularly feature examples from the Third World and other countries as well as Europe.

Delegation Interministerielle à la Ville (1990). *148 Quartiers.* Paris: Delegation à L' Amenagement Du Territoire et à L'Action Regionale.

Duggan, Carmel and Ronayne, Tom (1991). *Working Partners? The State and the Community Sector.* Dublin: Work Research Centre.

European Communities - Commission (1991). *The Regions in the 1990s - Fourth Periodic Report on the Social and Economic Situation.* Luxembourg: Office for the Official Publications of the EC.

Fogarty, Michael P. *(1986) Meeting the Needs of the Elderly.* Dublin: EFILWC.

Froessler, Rolf (1990). *The Renewal of the Third Town.* Dortmund: University of Dortmund Instituut fur Raumplanung.

Giaconi, Nicola and Vitali, Claudio (1990). *Coping with Social and Economic Change at Neighbourhood Level: Overview of the Situation in Italy.* Milan and Rome, Scuola di Psicosociologia Dell'organizzazione.

Grahl, John and Teague, Paul (1990). *1992, The Big Market*, London: Lawrence and Wishart.

Harvey, Brian (1992). *Networking in Europe: a Guide to European Voluntary Organisations.* London: CDF/NCVO (autumn).

Hiernaux, J P (1989). *Promoting Community Development in Europe - Results and Prospects of the Transnational Exchange of Experiences in the Field.* European Poverty Programme, Organisation and Dissemination Unit. Luxembourg: Office for Official Publications of the European Communities.

Jacquier, Claude (1990). *Programme of European Exchanges on the Revitalisation of Areas in Crisis.* Brussels: Commission of the European Communities (DGV).

Keppelhoff-Wiechert, Mrs Hedwig (1991). *Report on the Assessment of Women's Unwaged Work.* European Parliament, Commitee on Women's Rights.

Layton-Henry, Zig (1990). *The Political Rights of Migrant Workers in Western Europe.* London: Sage.

LEDA (1990). *Local Employment Development: Lessons from the LEDA*

*Programme.* Brussels, Commission of the European Communities.

Lipsky, M. and Smith, S R (1989-90). 'Nonprofit organisations, government and the welfare state'. *Political Science Quarterly*, 104:4.

McConnell, Charlie, ed. (1991) *A Citizens' Europe? Community Development in Europe, Towards 1992.* London: Community Development Foundation.

McConnell, Charlie (1991). *Promoting Community Development in Europe.* London: Community Development Foundation.

Mies, Maria (1986). *Patriarchy and Accumulation on a World Scale: Women in the International Division of Labour.* London and New Jersey, Zed Books.

O hUiginn, Padraig (1991). *Area-Based Response to Long-Term Unemployment.* Dublin: Programme for Economic and Social Progress.

Pickup, Laurie (1990). *Mobility and Social Cohesion in the European community - A Forward Look.* Dublin: EFILWC.

Programme Observation du Changement Social (1986). *L'Esprit des Lieux: Localites et Changement Social en France.* Paris: Editions du Centre National de la Recherche Scientifique.

Pronk, M (1990). *A World of Difference.* 's-Gravenhage: Voorlichtingsdienst Ontwikkelingssamenwerking van het ministerie van Buitenlandse Zaken

Rivault, Nathalie (1990). *Guide des Actions de la DGV dans les Domaines de l'Insertion Economique et Sociale.* Brussels: Commission of the European Communities.

Ronayne, Tom et al. (1989). *Coping with Social and Economic Change at Neighbourhood Level, Research Plan.* Dublin: EFILWC.

Room, Graham (1990). *'New Poverty' in the European Community.* London: Macmillan.

Shiva, Vandana (1989). *Staying Alive: Women, Ecology and Development.* London and New Jersey: Zed Books.

Sivandan et al, eds. (1991). 'Europe: variations on a theme of racism'. *Race and Class* 32:3, Jan-March.

Smith, Steven Rathgeb (1990). *Managing the Community: Privatisation, Government and the Nonprofit Sector.* Paper delivered at annual meeting of the American Political Science association, San Francisco, Aug-Sept.

Stohr, W.B. (1989). *Global Challenge and Local Response.* Pre-publication.

Thomas, Andrew and Finch, Helen (1990). *On Volunteering: A Qualitative Study of Images, Motivations and Experiences.* Berkhamsted: The Volunteer Centre

Tocqueville, Alexis de (1835). *Democracy in America.* English translation by George Lawrence, New York: Collins, Fontana Library 1968.

Waring, Marilyn (1988). *If Women Counted.* London: Macmillan.

# *Selective index*

accountability 98-9, 111, 116-7, 120 - see also autonomy, control
action - see local community action
activists 83-4, 120 - see also volunteers
advice - see counselling
age differences 44, 46, 50, 85
amenities 48, 52, 73-5, 139
Amsterdam Mid-North - see Netherlands
arm's-length resourcing 135, 138, 148, 153 - see also control
arts - see culture
associations 15, 138 - see also community groups
authorities - see public services
autonomy (of local groups) viii, 10, 14-15, 67, 87, 95-100, 115, 117, 149, 152 and passim

Bannedok Patients' Society 78-80, 87, 101
Belgium vii, 5, 7, 14, 18-19, 33, 34, 42, 50, 61, 68, 72, 75, 84, 86, 89, 104-5, 110, 116-7, 130-1, 133-4, 141, 143
Bell 143
Berghman 143
Bethlenfalvy 91, 127
Boucneau, Decleir et al 5, 150
Brinson 93
Britain - see United Kingdom
Burton, Forest and Stewart 2
business - see Social Partners

Can Serra - see Spain
Chanan and Vos 5, 95
charities - see voluntary sector
children 75, 86-8, 106, 129, 139, 144
church 4, 13, 14, 107-8 - see also religious groups
citizens 10, 11, 16, 92, 137 - see also local community
Citizens' Advice Bureau 54, 61
Combat Poverty Agency 97
Commission of the European Communities 126, 140 - see also European Community
community centres - see premises
community groups viii, 7, 9, 46-55, 59-63, 65-108, 118-19, 140, 143, 155 and passim
community development viii, 43, 102-4, 110, 115, 142-3, 150-2, 155 - see also umbrella groups

*161*

Community Development Journal 92
community work - see community development
consultation 101, 103, 111, 117, 130, 149
consumers 119
contracts 99, 100-2, 112, 116, 133, 135, 148-9, 153 - see also funding
control 14, 101, 103, 111, 114-5, 117-23, 131, 136 - see also accountability, autonomy
co-operation - see networking
co-operatives 81, 88
co-ordination - see integrated approach
Council of Europe 150
counselling 61
culture 47-9, 92-3, 104-6, 111, 136

decentralisation 104, 115-6, 131-2, 135
definitions 3, 11-16
Delegation Interministerielle a la Ville 127
democracy 75, 89, 95, 102, 111, 115, 117, 122-3, 135, 138
dependence 96, 117 - see also autonomy
deprivation 9, 85, 151, 155 - see also poverty
De Tocqueville epigraph, 117-18
development viii, 101, 117, 126, 128, 136, 142 - see also community development and passim
disadvantage - see poverty

EC - see European Community
ecology - see environment
Economic and Social Committee 129, 151
economy - see employment, and unpaid work
education 61, 73-5, 78, 87, 100, 153 - see also social issues
elderly 54, 77, 86, 104, 139, 144
employment 2, 6, 51, 71, 77, 86, 90, 106, 112, 144, 146 - see also social issues
environment 6, 38, 73, 93, 112, 152 - see also social issues
ethnic minorities and groups 42, 65, 75, 85, 88-93, 100, 154 - see also migrants
European Community vii, 2, 10, 125-130, 133, 144, 146, 151, 155
European Foundation for the Improvement of Living and Working Conditions v, 1, 2, 90
evaluation 74-77, 134, 151
exclusion 85, 140-1 - see also isolation, participation, poverty
externally-led groups viii, 15, 100, 110 - see also autonomy

facilities - see amenities
flexibility 112, 114, 120, 141, 147
Fogarty 86
France vii, 11, 127
friends, relatives and neighbours viii, 14, 35, 50, 57 62, 66, 134
Froessler 151
funding 14, 70-1, 99-103, 105, 111-12, 118-23, 132-4, 139, 148, 152,

154 - see also resources

gender 44-6, 50, 61-2, 65, 144-6 - see also women
Germany vii, 151
grants - see funding
Greece vii, 5, 7, 11, 20-21, 33, 34, 41, 66, 68, 72, 76, 87, 89, 106, 109-10, 113, 130-2, 134-5, 137
groups - see community groups
Gypsies - see travellers

Harvey 15
health 6, 61, 71, 74, 78-9, 86-7, 112 - see also social issues
helpers - see volunteers
Hiernaux 3
Holland see Netherlands
homeless 2 - see also housing
Home Tuition Project 100
households v, 3-4, 13, 87, 139-40, 144 and passim
household survey 6, 33-63
housing 6, 61, 73-5, 79, 112 - see also social issues

inactivity 129, 154 - see also unpaid work
information 79, 85, 99, 103, 108, 132, 139, 149 - see also umbrella groups
institutions 114, 127-8
integrated approach 3, 116, 127, 133 - see also partnership
intermediary bodies - see umbrella groups
International Union of Local Authorities 109
intervention 1, 8, 10, 128 and passim
involvement vii, 51, 58, 110, 126 - see also participation, and passim
Ireland vii, 5, 7, 22-23, 33, 34, 39, 42, 51, 62, 68, 72, 76-7, 87, 108, 115, 130-3, 136
isolation 54-7, 85, 88, 144, 153 - see also exclusion
issues - see social issues
Italy vii, 73, 79

Jacquier 128-9

Keppelhoff-Wiechert 90

language 29, 75, 100
Layton-Henry 91
length of residence 36, 45-6, 50
living conditions 152 and passim - see also neighbourhoods and problems
local action - see local community action
local authorities - see public services
local branches 15 - see also voluntary sector
local community
    - action 1, 3, 10, 43, 55, 126-8, 130, 135, 138, 152 and passim
    - groups - see community groups
    - sector 3, 9, 13, 65, 67-70, 128-9, 140, 147-50, 153, 155
local voluntary sector - see voluntary sector

*163*

Lomé agreement  92

Maastricht Treaty  3, 129
management  99, 106, 114, 137, 139
McConnell  150
Meet a Mum  85, 88
men  88-90 - see also gender
method  5-7, 66, 148-151
Mies  144
migrant populations  54, 89-93, 117, 127 - see also ethnic
mobility  74, 146
Moroccan Cultural Organisation  89
municipalities - see also public services

national voluntary organisations  81, 97, 104-5, 139, 154 - see also voluntary sector
neighbourhood  5, 34, 56, 137, 139 - and passim
Neighbourhoods in Crisis  128
neighbours - see friends, relatives and neighbours
Netherlands  vii, 5, 7, 8, 24-5, 33, 34, 42, 61, 69, 72, 74, 85, 87, 89, 98, 104, 111, 130, 132, 134, 141
networks  viii, 1, 67, 70, 99, 102-5, 122-3, 137, 139, 148 - see also umbrella groups
Non Governmental Organisations  93 - see also voluntary organisations

Oliveira do Douro - see Portugal

paid staff - see professional staff
parents  2, 73, 88-9, 106 - see also children, education
participation  viii, 1, 9, 47, 83-5, 97-8, 102, 111, 116, 120, 126-8, 135, 141, 143 and passim
partnership  viii, 1, 3, 11, 15, 100-2, 114, 119-25, 128-9, 149, 154
Perama - see Greece
peripherality  6, 34,
planning  73-4, 79, 107, 151-2
policy-making  viii, 7, 66, 101, 109-23, 132, 136 and passim
political parties  13, 49, 67, 97, 118
pollution  75 - see also environment
Portugal  vi, vii, 4, 5, 7, 11, 26-7, 33-4, 40, 60, 65, 69, 72, 76, 82, 84, 87, 105, 111, 113, 130-1, 136-7, 145
poverty  v, vi, 1, 54, 85-6, 90, 117, 126, 129-30, 140-3, 147 - see also deprivation, exclusion, isolation and passim
Poverty Programme  3, 21, 90, 110, 152
premises  99, 103, 107-8, 155 - see also resources, umbrella groups
problems in localities  4, 43ff, 101, 120 132, 139-40, 147 and passim
professional staff (in voluntary organisations)  97-100, 102, 105, 110, 116, 123, 128, 135, 137
professional voluntary organisations  15, 111 - see also voluntary sector
project culture  viii, 126-7, 133, 153
Proletarian Cultural Centre  79, 81

*164*

Pronk 93, 95
public authorities - see public services
publicity 51, 100
public services ix, 2, 9, 11, 13, 48, 57, 74, 84, 101, 108-11, 114-15, 118, 120-3, 126, 132, 136, 138-40, 147 and passim

quantification 77ff, 83, 87

race - see ethnic and migrant
refugees 90, 93
regions 10, 126, 129, 146, 151-2
relatives - see friends, relatives and neighbours
religious groups 47, 49, 52, 67, 97, 104
resources 14, 96-101, 120-3, 129, 137, 140, 147, 149 - see also funding
road safety - see transport
Ronayne, Duggan et al 5

safety 75 - see also transport
sample (household survey) 33ff
satisfaction (with recourses for problems) 57ff, (with volunteering) 84
schools - see education
self-help groups 48, 75, 127 - see also community groups
semi-autonomous groups 15, 17, 98, 100, 105 - see also autonomy
sex differences - see gender and women
Shiva 146
Single European Act 2
Single European Market 2
Sluizeken and Muide - see Belgium
Smith 116
Social Action Programmes vii, 2, 126, 129, 152
Social Charter 3
social cohesion 2, 76, 96,112, 128, 140, 152 and passim
social issues viii, 6, 38, 40 and passim - see also transport, housing, education, environment, health, employment,
Social Partners 4, 13, 74, 110, 118, 123, 134, 149, 155 - see also trade unions, commerce
social welfare - see welfare
Spain vii, 5, 7, 28-29, 33, 34, 39, 41, 50, 60, 69, 72, 75-6, 87-8, 107, 111, 119, 131, 134
sport 47, 49, 52, 66, 105-6
stability 146
statistics 10, 139
Stohr 96
strategy ix, 4, 103, 110-11, 118, 125, 127, 130-5, 140-2, 146-8, 153
Structural Funds vi, 2, 126, 129
subsidiarity 131-2
subsidy - see funding
suffrage 117 - see also democracy

Tallaght - see Ireland

*165*

telephones 55-7, 88, 104, 154
Thamesmead - see United Kingdom
Thamesmead Advisory Forum 103
Third Equality Programme 86
Third World 92, 144
Thomas and Finch 96
Thuishaven Centre for the Elderly 102
Tocqueville - see De Tocqueville
trade unions 4, 13, 75 - see also Social Partners
traffic - see transport
training 6, 73, 75, 77-8, 104, 106, 136 - see also education
transport 6, 38, 55, 66, 73-5, 85, 104, 146, 152
travellers 92
Trust Thamesmead 103

UK - see United Kingdom
umbrella groups v, 52, 70, 100, 102-8, 118, 136-7, 141, 148, 155
Unemployed Shipyard Workers' Organisation 85
unemployment - see employment
United Kingdom vi, vii, 5, 7, 15, 30-31, 33, 36, 41, 51, 61, 69, 72, 83, 85, 100-5, 111, 129-30, 135, 137, 141
United Nations System of National Accounting 90
United States 116
unpaid work 90, 96, 119-21, 129, 139, 154 - see also volunteers
urbanisation 34, 73, 79

Vietnamese 100
Vogelburt and IJ-Plein Working Group 75
voluntary organisations - see voluntary sector and national voluntary organisations
voluntary sector ix, 3-4, 13-16, 71, 86, 103, 115, 121-3, 130-1, 138-41, 148-9 - see also local community sector
volunteers 81, 83, 87, 96, 99, 121 - see also voluntary sector and passim

Waring 90, 144
welfare 85-6, 109, 116, 131, 136 and passim
women 6, 41, 77, 86-90, 96-9, 105, 119 - see also gender
Wrexham 143

youth 46, 75, 104

European Communities — Commission

**Out of the Shadows**

Luxembourg: Office for Official Publications of the European Communities, 1992

1992 — 190 pp. — 23.5 × 16 cm

ISBN 92-826-4146-5

Price (excluding VAT) in Luxembourg: ECU 15.00

# Venta y suscripciones • Salg og abonnement • Verkauf und Abonnement • Πωλήσεις και συνδρομές
# Sales and subscriptions • Vente et abonnements • Vendita e abbonamenti
# Verkoop en abonnementen • Venda e assinaturas

## BELGIQUE / BELGIË

**Moniteur belge /
Belgisch Staatsblad**
Rue de Louvain 42 / Leuvenseweg 42
1000 Bruxelles / 1000 Brussel
Tél. (02) 512 00 26
Fax 511 01 84
CCP / Postrekening 000-2005502-27

Autres distributeurs /
Overige verkooppunten

**Librairie européenne/
Europese Boekhandel**
Avenue Albert Jonnart 50 /
Albert Jonnartlaan 50
1200 Bruxelles / 1200 Brussel
Tél. (02) 734 02 81
Fax 735 08 60

**Jean De Lannoy**
Avenue du Roi 202 /Koningslaan 202
1060 Bruxelles / 1060 Brussel
Tél. (02) 538 51 69
Télex 63220 UNBOOK B
Fax (02) 538 08 41

**CREDOC**
Rue de la Montagne 34 / Bergstraat 34
Bte 11 / Bus 11
1000 Bruxelles / 1000 Brussel

## DANMARK

**J. H. Schultz Information A/S
EF-Publikationer**
Ottiliavej 18
2500 Valby
Tlf. 36 44 22 66
Fax 36 44 01 41
Girokonto 6 00 08 86

## BR DEUTSCHLAND

**Bundesanzeiger Verlag**
Breite Straße
Postfach 10 80 06
5000 Köln 1
Tel. (02 21) 20 29-0
Telex ANZEIGER BONN 8 882 595
Fax 20 29 278

## GREECE/ΕΛΛΑΔΑ

**G.C. Eleftheroudakis SA**
International Bookstore
Nikis Street 4
10563 Athens
Tel. (01) 322 63 23
Telex 219410 ELEF
Fax 323 98 21

## ESPAÑA

**Boletín Oficial del Estado**
Trafalgar, 27
28010 Madrid
Tel. (91) 44 82 135

**Mundi-Prensa Libros, S.A.**
Castelló, 37
28001 Madrid
Tel. (91) 431 33 99 (Libros)
431 32 22 (Suscripciones)
435 36 37 (Dirección)
Télex 49370-MPLI-E
Fax (91) 575 39 98

Sucursal:

**Libreria Internacional AEDOS**
Consejo de Ciento, 391
08009 Barcelona
Tel. (93) 301 86 15
Fax (93) 317 01 41

**Llibreria de la Generalitat
de Catalunya**
Rambla dels Estudis, 118 (Palau Moja)
08002 Barcelona
Tel. (93) 302 68 35
302 64 62
Fax (93) 302 12 99

## FRANCE

**Journal officiel
Service des publications
des Communautés européennes**
26, rue Desaix
75727 Paris Cedex 15
Tél. (1) 40 58 75 00
Fax (1) 40 58 75 74

## IRELAND

**Government Supplies Agency**
4-5 Harcourt Road
Dublin 2
Tel. (1) 61 31 11
Fax (1) 78 06 45

## ITALIA

**Licosa Spa**
Via Duca di Calabria, 1/1
Casella postale 552
50125 Firenze
Tel. (055) 64 54 15
Fax 64 12 57
Telex 570466 LICOSA I
CCP 343 509

## GRAND-DUCHÉ DE LUXEMBOURG

**Messageries Paul Kraus**
11, rue Christophe Plantin
2339 Luxembourg
Tél. 499 88 88
Télex 2515
Fax 499 88 84 44
CCP 49242-63

## NEDERLAND

**SDU Overheidsinformatie**
Externe Fondsen
Postbus 20014
2500 EA 's-Gravenhage
Tel. (070) 37 89 911
Fax (070) 34 75 778

## PORTUGAL

**Imprensa Nacional**
Casa da Moeda, EP
Rua D. Francisco Manuel de Melo, 5
1092 Lisboa Codex
Tel. (01) 69 34 14

**Distribuidora de Livros
Bertrand, Ld.ª**
**Grupo Bertrand, SA**
Rua das Terras dos Vales, 4-A
Apartado 37
2700 Amadora Codex
Tel. (01) 49 59 050
Telex 15798 BERDIS
Fax 49 60 255

## UNITED KINGDOM

**HMSO Books (PC 16)**
HMSO Publications Centre
51 Nine Elms Lane
London SW8 5DR
Tel. (071) 873 2000
Fax GP3 873 8463
Telex 29 71 138

## ÖSTERREICH

**Manz'sche Verlags-
und Universitätsbuchhandlung**
Kohlmarkt 16
1014 Wien
Tel. (0222) 531 61-0
Telex 11 25 00 BOX A
Fax (0222) 531 61-39

## SUOMI

**Akateeminen Kirjakauppa**
Keskuskatu 1
PO Box 128
00101 Helsinki
Tel. (0) 121 41
Fax (0) 121 44 41

## NORGE

**Narvesen information center**
Bertrand Narvesens vei 2
PO Box 6125 Etterstad
0602 Oslo 6
Tel. (2) 57 33 00
Telex 79668 NIC N
Fax (2) 68 19 01

## SVERIGE

**BTJ**
Box 200
22100 Lund
Tel. (046) 18 00 00
Fax (046) 18 01 25

## SCHWEIZ / SUISSE / SVIZZERA

**OSEC**
Stampfenbachstraße 85
8035 Zürich
Tel. (01) 365 54 49
Fax (01) 365 54 11

## CESKOSLOVENSKO

**NIS**
Havelkova 22
13000 Praha 3
Tel. (02) 235 84 46
Fax 42-2-264775

## MAGYARORSZÁG

**Euro-Info-Service**
Budapest I. Kir.
Attila út 93
1012 Budapest
Tel. (1) 56 82 11
Telex (22) 4717 AGINF H-61
Fax (1) 17 59 031

## POLSKA

**Business Foundation**
ul. Krucza 38/42
00-512 Warszawa
Tel. (22) 21 99 93, 628-28-82
International Fax&Phone
(0-39) 12-00-77

## JUGOSLAVIJA

**Privredni Vjesnik**
Bulevar Lenjina 171/XIV
11070 Beograd
Tel. (11) 123 23 40

## CYPRUS

**Cyprus Chamber of Commerce and Industry**
Chamber Building
38 Grivas Dhigenis Ave
3 Deligiorgis Street
PO Box 1455
Nicosia
Tel. (2) 449500/462312
Fax (2) 458630

## TÜRKIYE

**Pres Gazete Kitap Dergi
Pazarlama Dağitim Ticaret ve sanay
AŞ**
Narlibahçe Sokak N. 15
Istanbul-Cağaloğlu
Tel. (1) 520 92 96 - 528 55 66
Fax 520 64 57
Telex 23822 DSVO-TR

## CANADA

**Renouf Publishing Co. Ltd**
Mail orders — Head Office:
1294 Algoma Road
Ottawa, Ontario K1B 3W8
Tel. (613) 741 43 33
Fax (613) 741 54 39
Telex 0534783

Ottawa Store:
61 Sparks Street
Tel. (613) 238 89 85

Toronto Store:
211 Yonge Street
Tel. (416) 363 31 71

## UNITED STATES OF AMERICA

**UNIPUB**
4611-F Assembly Drive
Lanham, MD 20706-4391
Tel. Toll Free (800) 274 4888
Fax (301) 459 0056

## AUSTRALIA

**Hunter Publications**
58A Gipps Street
Collingwood
Victoria 3066

## JAPAN

**Kinokuniya Company Ltd**
17-7 Shinjuku 3-Chome
Shinjuku-ku
Tokyo 160-91
Tel. (03) 3439-0121

Journal Department
PO Box 55 Chitose
Tokyo 156
Tel. (03) 3439-0124

AUTRES PAYS
OTHER COUNTRIES
ANDERE LÄNDER

**Office des publications officielles
des Communautés européennes**
2, rue Mercier
2985 Luxembourg
Tél. 49.92.81
Télex PUBOF LU 1324 b
Fax 48 85 73/48 68 17
CC bancaire BIL 8-109/6003/700

12.91